Television Drama in the Age of Streaming

Vilde Schanke Sundet

Television Drama in the Age of Streaming

Transnational Strategies and Digital Production
Cultures at the NRK

Vilde Schanke Sundet
Department of Media and Communication
University of Oslo
Oslo, Norway

Vilde Schanke Sundet has received support from the Norwegian Non-Fiction Writers and Translators Association for this publication.

ISBN 978-3-030-66417-6   ISBN 978-3-030-66418-3   (eBook)
https://doi.org/10.1007/978-3-030-66418-3

Cover pattern © Melisa Hasan

This Palgrave Pivot imprint is published by the registered company Springer Nature Switzerland AG.
The registered company address is: Gewerbestrasse 11, 6330 Cham, Switzerland

ACKNOWLEDGEMENTS

This book is the result of several years of research on changes within the television industry, including more detailed studies of digital production cultures, online drama and fan cultures. It started as postdoctoral fellowship as part of the 'Success in the Film and Television Industry' project (SiFTI, hosted by the Lillehammer University College), was extended with grants from the same university and the Norwegian Non-Fiction Writers and Translators Association, before it was finished as part of my work on the 'Streaming the Cultural Industries' project (STREAM, hosted by the University of Oslo). I want to thank all the institutions mentioned above for allowing me to write this book. During the years of writing, I have been associated with international research projects which widened my perspective. Most notably are 'What Makes Danish TV Drama Series Travel' (hosted by the University of Aarhus) and 'Reaching Young Audiences: Serial Fiction and Cross-Media Storyworlds for Children and Young Audiences' (hosted by the University of Copenhagen).

The empirical basis of the book builds on insight gained through extensive observations, interviews and discussions with industry experts and television fans. In total, the book builds on more than hundred interviews, hundreds of hours of observation, unique access to industry conferences, meetings, working documents and ratings, as well as a significant number of informal talks and discussions with both industry experts and fans. I am deeply thankful for the time and energy everyone has given me. I am particularly indebted to Knut Næsheim, Åse Marie Hole and the rest of the blank team at the NRK for allowing me to observe the making of an online drama for more than a year, with an unusual open attitude towards an outside researcher. I also like to thank Julie Andem, Kim Erlandsen, Marianne Furevold-Boland, Mari Magnus, Jan Strande Ødegårdstuen, Keld Reinicke, Håkon Lund Sørensen, Nils Petter Strømmen and Ida Sagmo Tvedte for fruitful discussions on television trends and digital storytelling. They have all been essential for my line of thought.

I am also grateful to scholars and colleagues who have inspired me. Most importantly, I want to thank Line Nybro Petersen, with whom I conducted the *SKAM*-fan study, which includes nearly fifty in-depth interviews with Scandinavian first-time fans. What a wonderful project! I also want to thank Mads Møller Tommerup Andersen, Matt Hills, Karoline Andrea Ihlebæk, Marika Lüders, Janet McCabe, Eva Novrup Redvall, Kari Steen-Johnsen, Jeanette Steemers, Trine Syvertsen, Anne Marit Waade, Espen Ytreberg and the STREAM-team (besides already mentioned Marika, Terje Colbjørnsen, Håvard Kiberg, Arnt Maasø and Hendrik Spilker) for insightful discussions and input, through either co-writing related articles with me, reading parts or the entire manuscript, or discussing the material.

Nils A. Nadeau proofread the manuscript, for which I am deeply thankful. I also want to thank Camille Davids, Jack Heeney and Shaun Vigil at Palgrave for taking this project on board and organising everything so neatly. Finally, I want to thank Anders, Kajsa and Jenny for loving watching television almost as much as me.

CONTENTS

LIST OF FIGURES

LIST OF TABLES

CHAPTER 1

National Television, Drama and Streaming

Abstract This chapter frames the book's ambition to analyse how new streaming services and incumbent television providers intersect and act in a new drama landscape, and how streaming impacts existing television production cultures, publishing models and industry–audience relations. It summarises the empirical case underpinning the book—an in-depth study of the Norwegian public service broadcaster (NRK) and some of its game-changing drama productions (e.g. *Lilyhammer*, *SKAM* and *blank*)— and describes its analytical approach of combining perspectives from production studies, media industry studies and fan studies. The study builds on insight gained through more than a hundred interviews with television experts and fans, hundreds of hours of observations and unique access to industry conferences, meetings, working documents and ratings.

Keywords NRK • Production cultures • Public service broadcasting • Streaming • Television drama • Television studies

© The Author(s), under exclusive license to Springer Nature Switzerland AG 2021
V. S. Sundet, *Television Drama in the Age of Streaming*,
https://doi.org/10.1007/978-3-030-66418-3_1

Introduction

Streaming is changing the television industry. In the trade press, a common descriptor for the new era of television is the 'streaming wars' (Klebnikov 2020; Sepinwall 2020), wherein global streaming services are throwing money at transnational drama series—increasing both budgets and production values—to the consternation of those wondering about how it all will affect national drama producers and broadcasters. Relatedly, many in the media worries that streaming will make the audience increasingly 'unfaithful' to national channels and broadcasters, in that people easily jump to digital platforms and international streaming services if they like what they find there. One television executive insisted that streaming fosters new relationships with the audience which leave the old 'love affair' with broadcast television behind. New drama strategies, he said, are now required: 'I don't think the love affair has ended, but it has met some challenges we must take seriously. We must understand that we don't get anything for free anymore—we used to, but we don't anymore' (Wallace interviewed 2015). Clearly, for him, streaming is not simply a question of new distribution technology or business models but an almost existential crisis for traditional media.

This book addresses television drama in the age of streaming—a time when television has been reshaped for national and international consumption via both linear 'flow' and on-demand user modes. Drawing upon the formative first decade of television streaming (2010–2019), the book looks at how global streaming services (such as Netflix, HBO, Amazon Prime and Disney Plus) and social media platforms (such as YouTube, Instagram, Facebook and TikTok) have impacted the assumptions of traditional television drama and prompted national broadcasters and producers to rethink their existing models and strategies. As such, the book analyses and discusses recent trends within the industry in terms of the production and release of television drama, as well as the relationships among industry players—national and international, public and private—and between the industry and its audience. A key argument is that television streaming brings with it both new opportunities and new challenges for drama producers and broadcasters and that these players must capitalise upon or confront these challenges and opportunities to remain viable. While incumbent national broadcasters (including public service institutions) often emphasise the challenging aspects of streaming (such as changing user habits and increasing competition), streaming also brings new storytelling techniques, flexible publishing models, better access to international markets and new forms of industry–audience relations. This book explores how and why these industry changes take place and what their implications may be.

A second key argument of the book is that the effect of television streaming cannot be adequately addressed on a general level, but has to be studied and addressed within its specific national and cultural context. As such, I concur with the argument of Gunn Enli and Trine Syvertsen (2016) that contextual factors are still essential for understanding television change and so is the position and strategic response of existing television institutions (see also Pertierra and Turner 2013; Lobato 2019). This book examines the way in which new streaming services and incumbent television provides meet and act in a Nordic cultural context unlike those that typically frame the streaming debate (Hills et al. 2019; Johnson 2018, 2019; Lotz 2018).

While streaming affects the television industry in a variety of ways, this book concentrates on its impact within the particular field of *television drama*. The growth of streaming services has led to significant demand for content, turning drama into an excellent driver of sales (Steemers 2016; see also Lotz 2007) and a priority area for streaming players positioning themselves to meet 'the future of television' (Shaw 2019). Drama is also a battlefield on which the competition has been particularly harsh (Littleton and Low 2019). In general, then, contemporary television drama is enjoying renewed significance to the extent that scholars, producers and critics alike are talking about a 'new' golden age (McElroy and Noonan 2019: 24; see also Waade et al. 2020b). And it is a particularly effective vehicle with which to study how streaming impacts production and publishing models, as well as power structures.

ANALYTICAL POSITIONING: PRODUCTION, INDUSTRY AND FANS

Studies of television streaming cut across various fields and disciplines including television studies, media industry studies, production studies, audience and fan studies, and studies of innovation, policy and economy. This book draws on insight from all these fields, but its argument is situated mainly in production studies, media industry studies and fan studies.

Production studies is grounded in the assumption that media products are informed by the context in which they are produced—that is, the people creating them, the institutions or companies where those people work, the industry to which they all belong and the larger structures of governmental policy and socioeconomic conditions which also frame this work (Banks 2014: 120; see also Banks et al. 2015; Mayer et al. 2009b; Paterson et al. 2016). A key argument within production studies is that media production itself is a form of culture, in the sense that producers share and develop norms and values, identities and practices (Caldwell 2008). Production practices are regarded as interpretations of ideas, values and beliefs, which means they develop uniquely across production cultures and structures (Levine 2001). Many studies combine larger perspectives upon structures and power dynamics with the analysis of production processes at the micro-level, highlighting how the day-to-day practices and decision-making of industry workers impact television production (Mayer et al. 2009a: 4). This 'production perspective' approaches television practices and motivations from the bottom up (Te Walvaart 2020).

Media industry studies is similar to production studies but aims to grasp broader industry shifts, including how media productions operate within fields where various competing institutions all struggle to stabilise structures that serve their specific interests (Havens et al. 2009: 250; see also Holt and Perren 2009). Daniel Herbert and his colleagues describe media industry studies as a 'big tent' of approaches focused on '*how individuals, institutions, and industries produce and circulate cultural forms in historically and geographically contextualized ways*' (2020: 7; italics in original). Relatedly, Timothy Havens and Amanda D. Lotz propose their 'industrialization of culture framework' (2020: 4–5) to unpack the various structures—or cultures—defining television production. They find that the production of media is interrelated with 'texts', 'the public' and broader 'social trends, tastes and traditions', all guided by three levels of influence: 'mandates', 'conditions' and 'practices' (2020: 6–9). 'Culture', however, forms the backdrop of their entire framework, suggesting its pervasive impact upon those mandates, conditions and practices.

Fan studies is grounded in the interest in fans and fandoms as a sociocultural phenomenon largely associated with modern capitalist societies, electronic media, mass culture and public performance (Duffett 2017). Fans can be defined as 'individuals who maintain a passionate connection to popular media, assert their identity through their engagement with and mastery over its contents, and experience social affiliation around shared tastes and preferences' (Jenkins 2016). Several such studies have addressed the emotional investment of television fans (Jenkins 1992; Jensen 1992; Hills 2002; Sandvoss 2005; Williams 2015) and how sharing these emotions with others drives the creation of fan spaces (Harrington and Bielby 1995; see also Baym 2000; Cavicchi 1998). A growing corpus of literature also addresses television fans' means of coping with digital and social media in transmedia narratives and how this engagement and connectedness both strengthens and deepens the television-viewing experience (Evans 2011, 2020; Jenkins 2006).

Production studies, media industry studies and fan studies have expanded significantly in number and scope over the past ten years and have often been successfully combined in broader analyses of recent television trends (see, e.g. Gray 2010; Gray and Lotz 2012; Havens and Lotz 2012; Holt and Sanson 2014; Hills et al. 2019; Jenkins 2006; Jenkins et al. 2013). In fact, among the Nordic countries, the combined model has informed several large-scale research projects and resulted in a Nordic approach to investigating the change in television and its effect on producers, audiences and industries.[1] The distinct and multifaceted approach of these projects views change in television through the lenses of recent drama success stories and the public service production cultures which drive these successes. It also engages industry–audience relations in ways which transcend the more traditional explanations of early television studies. For instance, Annette Hill (2019) uses the term 'push-pull dynamics' to describe how audiences' experience of media is connected to how producers craft content for audiences. She describes how cultural productions *push* audiences into content, 'for example through distribution and branding for television drama across live transmission or subscription services', and how audiences are *pulled* into storytelling, 'for example through strong characterization and multi-layered narratives in serial drama' (2019: 4). This push and pull between producers and audiences work both ways

[1] These projects include *Success in the Film and Television Industry: A Production Culture Perspective* (Lillehammer University College, 2013–2016), *Media Experiences* (Lund University, 2013–2016), *What Makes Television Drama Series Travel* (Aarhus University, 2014–2019), *Streaming the Culture Industries* (University of Oslo, 2017–2021) and *Reaching Young Audiences: Serial Fiction and Cross-Media Storyworlds for Children and Young Audiences* (Copenhagen University, 2019–2024). Several monographs and anthologies have been published as part of these projects, including Bakøy et al. 2016, 2017; Hansen and Waade 2017; Hill 2019; Jensen and Jacobsen 2020; Waade et al. 2020b. See also Andersen 2019; Bruun 2020; Redvall 2013 for related studies following a similar approach.

and are related to power. As Hill puts it, 'push-pull dynamics highlight what power looks like within the cultural production and reception of television' (2019: 5). The present study adopts this Nordic approach to address how streaming impacts not only the making of television drama but also the audience consumption of it and fan activities around it, all within the context of one particular broadcasting institution and some of its principal drama productions.

Television Streaming from a Test-Market Perspective

Studies of television streaming typically build on evidence from larger countries, predominantly from the Anglo-American sphere (Johnson 2018, 2019; Lotz 2018). This book contributes to the field by focusing on a Nordic country—Norway—characterised by a combination of high usage of global streaming services, but also high use of public service television and high demand for domestic content (Enli and Syvertsen 2016). Despite being one of the smaller markets in the world—Norway has a population of just five million people—it is nevertheless one of the most digitised and forward leaning in terms of its media consumption. The Norwegian market boasts a well-developed technological infrastructure which, combined with a relatively high Gross Domestic Product (GDP), allows most Norwegians both the opportunity and the means to explore new-media services.[2] Reports from Kantar Media confirm that younger Norwegian audiences (aged 12–19 years) are even more 'digitised' than their older counterparts (in terms of both time spent and services used) and that their consumption is increasingly devoted to international—rather than national—media services (Strømmen 2020). In this group, 97 per cent stream film and television and 94 per cent use social media on a daily basis (Sandvik et al. 2020: 15). Unsurprisingly, then, the Norwegian media market is commonly used as a strategic testing ground for many new-media services from national as well as international media players, and trends and strategies in this market are seen to anticipate those in other markets as well. The Norwegian experience, in short, transcends its national context in important media industry ways.

---

[2] In 2019, for example, 98 per cent of the population had internet access, 95 per cent had a smartphone, 72 per cent had access to a tablet and 69 per cent subscribed to one or more film and television streaming services (SSB 2020: 91).

NRK: 'A Gigantic Small Broadcaster'

This book relies on several complex examples and case studies to engage the media industry shift from linear 'flow' television to on-demand and online streaming services, starting with the efforts of the Norwegian public service broadcaster (NRK) and including some of its game-changing drama productions. NRK was originally launched as a publicly funded national radio broadcaster in 1933 along the lines of the British BBC and many other public service institutions in Western Europe (Syvertsen 2004); it added television to its services in 1960. Although private and commercial cable and satellite channels were introduced in Norway in the late 1980s, NRK retained its national broadcasting monopoly until the early 1990s, when commercially funded television and radio institutions with similar public service obligations began to appear (Syvertsen 1997). NRK still holds a strong position compared to other national media players in Norway and operates the market-leading television and radio channels in addition to strong online news and streaming services. As of 2019, 89 per cent of the population used one or more of NRK's services on any given day (NRK 2020: 13), and this number was relatively stable across the entire ten years analysis period. As for its branding, NRK often describes itself as 'a gigantic small broadcaster' (Fordal 2015), referring to its relative impact within the limited Norwegian market. Still, NRK is increasingly confronting competition from both streaming platforms and social media providers, to which it is losing market shares, especially with younger age groups.

For a long time, NRK was almost alone in Norway to produce and commission television drama, due to these series' high budgets and complex production setups. Initially, NRK produced all its drama in house, but it was eventually obliged to increase its use of outside productions (Meld. St. 38 [2014–2015]). Today, NRK commissions and co-produces drama with a range of external production companies and co-production partners, both to fulfil political obligations and to pool creative ideas and increase budgets and markets (for an overview, see NRK 2019). At the same time, other broadcasters have increased their literal and figurative investments in television drama, and as of 2019, all the Norwegian broadcasters claim 'original' television drama to be a strategic priority (Kampanje 2019). During the ten-year analysis period, then, the Norwegian television drama market has transformed from a small-scale assortment of mostly NRK-produced series to a much wider variety of series produced by public and private, and national and international, players.

From Lilyhammer *to* SKAM *and* blank

This book engages in particular with the game-changing NRK drama productions *Lilyhammer* (Rubicon TV for NRK and Netflix, 2012–2014), *SKAM* (NRK, 2015–2017) and *blank* (NRK, 2018–2019). They are all vivid examples of the impact of streaming on television drama during the analysis period, and they are selected because they particularly well reflect key tendencies and trends within the Norwegian streaming television market.[3]

Lilyhammer is often referred to as Netflix's first original series, even though the Norwegian production company Rubicon TV (owned by Endemol Shine Group) produced it as an NRK/Netflix co-production. It was first pitched as an NRK-drama only, but Netflix entered as co-investor during the production of season 1. This production-set-up meant *Lilyhammer* was realised by players which differed greatly in audience scope (national vs international), business model (license fee vs pay TV), publishing model (linear vs on-demand) and distribution practice (broadcasting vs streaming). In addition to the international markets made available through Netflix, the distributor Red Arrow sold *Lillehammer* internationally, and its first season would eventually appear in 130 counters (Hansen 2013).

The storyline of *Lilyhammer* follows US mafia boss Frank Tagliano (played by Steven Van Zandt), who moves to the small Norwegian town of Lillehammer as part of a witness protection programme. Here he must start over on both a professional and a personal level. The series mixes elements of action, drama and comedy and plays with the Nordic noir genre (Creeber 2015). For instance, the storyline itself is layered, concerning both a mafia boss in hiding and the Norwegian welfare state as seen from a stereotypical US perspective. During the three seasons, there is a predictable clash between Norwegian and US values and cultures, and the first season, in

---

[3] I have analysed *Lilyhammer* and *SKAM* also in previous publications. Previous analyses of *Lilyhammer* include Sundet 2016 (*Still 'Desperately seeking the audience'? Audience making in the age of media convergence (the* Lilyhammer *experience)*) and Sundet 2017a (*Co-produced television drama and the cost of transnational 'success': The making of* Lilyhammer). Previous analyses of *SKAM* include Sundet 2017b (*'Det er bare du som kan føle det du føler'—emosjonell investering og engasjement i nettdramaet SKAM*), Sundet 2019 (*From 'secret' online teen drama to international cult phenomenon: The global expansion of SKAM and its public service mission*), and Andersen and Sundet 2019 (*Producing online youth fiction in a Nordic public-service context*). In this book, I see *Lilyhammer, SKAM* and *blank* in relation to each other and frame them within the overall context of streaming.

particular, is filled with commentary regarding the Norwegian way of life. This includes Tagliano's interaction with the Immigration and the Labour and Welfare Administration, and, after he starts a family, with the Norwegian health care system and its gender-equality measures, including a meeting with a male midwife and the Nordic concept of paternity leave.

The coming-of-age shows *SKAM* and *blank* both build on an online drama format developed by NRK specifically to target young girls. This format publishes the storyline daily and in real-time on a blog through a mix of video clips, chat messages and pictures. The format invites the audience to engage through comment sections. The format also draws upon extensive audience research to gain in-depth information on the targeted niche audience and to identify ways in which these series could serve their needs. Starting in 2018, the *SKAM* universe expanded through several remakes, among which the US version, titled *SKAM Austin* (XIX Entertainment for Facebook Watch, 2018–2019), is probably the best known (Carlström 2017; Donadio 2016).

The storyline of *SKAM* follows a cast of teenage characters as they navigate everyday life at home and school. Each season centres on a different main character from a first-person point of view: Season 1 follows Eva (played by Lisa Teige) who begins high school and has to navigate new social hierarchies while wondering about her boyfriend Jonas's (Marlon Langeland) commitment to her; season 2 follows Noora (played by Josefine Frida Pettersen) who falls in love with alpha male William (Thomas Hayes) while also struggling with a sexual assault; season 3 follows Isak (played by Tarjei Sandvik Moe) who has to come to terms with his sexuality after falling in love with the boy Even (played by Henrik Holm) while also dealing with his own prejudice against mental illness; and season 4 follows Sana (played by Iman Meskini) who has to balance her life with friends with her religious respect and belief. By mixing elements from drama, sitcom and soap opera, *SKAM* combined a complex TV narratology with humour and daily cliff-hangers (Faldalen 2016).

Like *SKAM*, the storyline of *blank* follows youth characters as they navigate their lives—told from a first-person point of view—but in this case the youths are slightly older (nineteen, not sixteen). Furthermore, in *blank*, each season follows a new character in a new universe: season 1 follows Ella (played by Cecilie Amlie Conesa) who struggle to find a direction for her new 'adult life' and dealing with a boyfriend she no longer loves; season 2 follows Zehra (played by Ayyüce Kozanli) as she fulfils her family's expectation of studying 'something sensible' while dreaming of making music, crossing different sociocultural environments along the way; and season 3 follows Markus (played by Alfred Ekker Strande) who moves back to his small home town after a year in the city and experience that nothing is as before. Also *blank* mixed elements from drama and soap opera, but followed a more documentary aesthetic, especially in the first season.

Figure 1.1 illustrates *Lilyhammer*, *SKAM* and *blank* as they are presented in NRK's online player.

Fig. 1.1   *Lilyhammer, SKAM* and *blank*

Fig. 1.1 (continued)

Both *Lilyhammer* and *SKAM* broke new ground in terms of audience ratings, amenability to international export and innovation in production and publishing models. *Lilyhammer* was promoted as Netflix's 'first original series' (despite being a co-production between NRK and Netflix) and a test case for Netflix's 'all-at-once-watching' model (Carr 2012), which in turn inspired NRK and others to introduce 'binge-watching' as a new publishing model for drama series. *SKAM* and its real-time online drama format challenged the concept of 'television drama' altogether, both at NRK and internationally (Stokel-Walker 2017). Its 'real-time' publishing meant that the time and date in the series followed the time and date of the audience, making its publishing rhythm irregular and unpredictable but also generating a sense of authenticity and liveness. In short, both *Lilyhammer* and *SKAM* are excellent examples of digital flagship productions (Sundet 2020), meaning that they served as change-makers within the streaming television industry, provided a model of new ways of operating, and gained renown and cultural impact through their market success. As *SKAM*'s successor, *blank* gives insight into the legacy of *SKAM* on a strategic and production level and provides an interesting comparison with its two precedents.

Table 1.1 gives an overview of the selected drama cases.

Table 1.1 Overview of selected drama cases (*Lilyhammer*, *SKAM* and *blank*)

	Lilyhammer (2012–2014)	*SKAM (2015–2017)*	*blank (2018–2019)*
Producer	Rubicon TV	NRK	NRK
Distributor	NRK/Netflix/Red Arrow (internationally)	NRK	NRK
Showrunner	Anne Bjørnstad and Eilif Skodvin (S1–S3)	Julie Andem (S1–S4)	Knut Næsheim (S1) Knut Næsheim with Karianne Lund (manuscript) and Mikael Hovland (directing) (S2–S3)
Seasons and episodes	S1: 8 episodes, 6 hours S2: 8 episodes, 6 hours S3: 8 episodes, 6 hours	S1: 11 episodes, 3 hours and 40 minutes S2: 12 episodes, 6 hours and 9 minutes S3: 10 episodes, 3 hours and 55 minutes S4: 10 episodes, 5 hours and 28 minutes	S1: 9 episodes, 4 hours and 4 minutes S2: 9 episodes, 3 hours and 16 minutes S3: 8 episodes, 3 hours and 46 minutes
International sales and remakes	Distributed through Netflix and sold by Red Arrow to 130 territories	Distributed in Scandinavia, produced as a remake in seven countries (France, Germany, United States (global distribution through Facebook Watch), Italy, Netherlands, Spain and Belgium)	Distributed in Scandinavia

Studying Digital Flagship Productions and Their Audiences and Fans

This book combines various methodological approaches and empirical sources to investigate television drama in the age of streaming, including, principally, in-depth cases studies of specific television dramas, interviews with key informants, ethnographic field observation, analysis of media artefacts and industry deep texts and, finally, analysis of audience ratings and statistics.

Interviews with Key Informants

Much of the empirical basis of this book builds on insights gained through extensive interviews and discussions with industry experts and television fans. In total, the book builds on more than one hundred semi-structured interviews, in addition to a lot of more informal talks and discussions. Fifty of the interviews were with industry professionals from the Norwegian television industry who were selected to represent creative and strategic roles in the three case studies, as well as other key decision-makers mostly working at NRK (see the appendix for an overview of the informants with titles and affiliations). These individuals should all be categorised as 'elites' (Hertz and Imber 1995) or 'exclusive informants' (Bruun 2016), meaning that they have a particularly relevant perspective upon the topic under scrutiny and that they cannot be easily replaced. For the *Lilyhammer* case, this group included showrunners, executive producers, commissioning editors, schedulers and others, not only from NRK but also from the production company Rubicon TV. For the *SKAM* case, this group included several members of the production team as well as other NRK informants who were impacted by *SKAM*'s success (including people working in format sales and legal rights). For the *blank* case, this group included the whole production team, as well as some of the actors, and many of them were interviewed more than once. In all the interviews, particular weight was given to the informants' 'self-reflexivity' (Caldwell 2009)—that is, their specific and unguided reflections on the key choices and strategies which were made. The interviews were conducted from spring 2015 to autumn 2019, thus spanning a crucial period of change both within the Norwegian television market and in drama production in general.

In addition to interviews with television professionals, the book also draws on in-depth interviews with fifty *SKAM* fans from the three Scandinavian countries (Norway, Denmark and Sweden) ranging from thirteen to seventy years old, which I conducted with Line Nybro Petersen.[4] The informants were self-recruited based on a call for participants in the larger Scandinavian *SKAM* fan groups on Facebook, as well as on a research blog during the last season of *SKAM* (spring 2017); the

---

[4] The informants included both genders and a wide age span, though most were women between thirty and fifty years old. Gender-wise, there were forty-four women and six men. Age-wise, they distributed as follows: under 20 years old: 5 people; 20–29: 5; 30–39: 13; 40–49: 19; 50–59: 6; 60 and over: 2. For other analysis based on this material, see Petersen and Sundet 2019; Sundet and Petersen 2020.

interviews took place the following autumn. Although the informants cannot be categorised as 'elites' or 'exclusive' in the ethnographic sense used above, they are in fact 'experts' with unique competence and knowledge about the topic. All the interviews followed the same semi-structured guide, including questions concerning how and why they entered *SKAM* fandom, experiences with being a *SKAM* fan, fan practices and the fan's afterlife when the show had ended. The informants were also invited to send us links to fan material which was either important to them or illustrative of their fan practices, such as fan posts, fan drawings, fan fiction or background information on fan activities and campaigns. While several of our informants were very public about being a fan, taking part in large fan groups and even earning some renown within the fandom, most expressed concern regarding how their fan identity would appear both within and outside the fan community, clearly preferring privacy over publicity. In this book, then, all the informants are anonymised in order to allow them to speak freely; attribution is by age and gender alone.[5]

Ethnographic Field Observation

The empirical basis of this book also builds on insight gained through extensive observation both within the television industry and within online fan communities following the selected drama productions. The aim here was to put together a 'thick description' (Geertz 1973) of the subject under scrutiny, adding context and complexity to interview statements and, importantly, developing and sharing intuitive understandings of both industry and fan practices. This work, in turn, increases the likelihood of asking sensible questions and conducting informed analyses in the research.

To start with, this book draws upon an extensive observation study of the *blank* production from August 2017 to August 2018, which encompassed the pre-production, production and publishing of season 1. That study was inspired by Eva Novrup Redvall's (2013) insightful production study of Danish television drama but took lessons from other television production studies as well, in which observation represents a key means of gaining insight into industry decision-making and practices. In all, my study of *blank* involved over 150 hours of observation spread across more than 60 days and including strategic and weekly team meetings, the writing and editing room, casting work and on-set activity. My approach was

---

[5] All interview quotations have been translated from Norwegian, Danish or Swedish into English by the author.

to 'look over the shoulders' of television workers to identify the interpretive and often taken-for-granted aspects of their practice (Caldwell 2009). Although my access had to be negotiated and specified, the production team was unusually open and welcoming—I was granted an admission card, given access to internal working documents and invited to decide for myself which meetings or parts of the production I was interested in observing. This availability is particularly noteworthy given that *blank* was the drama production which followed the hit show *SKAM*, and, as a result, it faced very high expectations from NRK itself, the public and the press. Because the production of *blank* involved numerous meetings with other NRK divisions as well, my observation study gave deep insight into not only the specifics of online drama and digital production cultures but also NRK's television strategies and production routines in general during a critical period.

In addition to the production study of *blank*, I also conducted a digital ethnography (Pink et al. 2016) of online fans and fan communities as part of my study of *SKAM* fans (some of whom turned into *blank* fans as well). More precisely, I followed the principal Scandinavian Facebook fan groups (Kosegruppa DK, SKAM Fri og Ekte) from autumn 2016 until autumn 2019, exploring how they developed both while *SKAM* was on the air and after the show ended, as well as how they responded to new online drama shows such as *blank*. Because online fan communities often sprawl across media platforms (Bore 2017; Stein 2015), I also followed these fans' activities on Tumblr, Jodel, Twitter, Instagram and YouTube. I concur wholeheartedly with Marika Lüders's claim that 'in order to draw an authentic image of online environments, *being* online is essential' (2007: 24).

Analysis of Media Artefacts and Industry Deep Texts

In addition to interviews and observation, this book also relies upon an analysis of the many artefacts and texts surrounding the television industry and the selected drama productions, including internal working documents (manuscripts, guidelines, schedules, etc.), institutional documents (describing missions and strategies), promo material, news articles in national and international newspapers and trade press, and fan-created content and materials. John T. Caldwell (2008) labels these sources 'media artefacts and industry deep texts' and argues for their value to any analysis of media production (see also Gray 2010). In this book, the artefacts and texts reflect all three levels in Caldwell's (2008) model, from fully embedded to semi-embedded to publicly disclosed.

Audience Ratings and Statistics

Lastly, this book relies on the analysis of audience ratings and statistics related to Norwegian television drama, with a particular focus on *Lilyhammer*, *SKAM* and *blank*. During analysis period, changes within the television industry affected not only the making and consumption of television drama but also the measurement of that consumption. In 2018, Norway introduced a new hybrid model for measuring both linear and on-demand streaming television and video into the official currency for television viewing (see Kantar 2016). In this book, I draw on audience insight from the official television survey, as well as statistics and analysis from NRK's division for audience insight, which conducts a great variety of studies concerning how audiences and fans engage with NRK's content. While these kinds of studies can be hard for an outside researcher to access, NRK was invariably open to my requests. Regarding the *blank* case, I even received unlimited access to the Google Analytics statistics for the show's website (blank.p3.no), which allowed me to follow the activity on the website daily and in real-time and thus gain a unique perspective on the audience's user habits.[6]

Table 1.2 gives an overview of the various methods used in the different production studies of this book.

Table 1.2 Overview of cases and sources (*Lilyhammer*, *SKAM* and *blank*)

	Lilyhammer (2012–2014)	*SKAM (2015–2017)*	*blank (2018–2019)*
Interviews with key informants	Interviews with industry professionals	Interviews with industry professionals Interview with *SKAM* fans	Interviews with industry professionals
Observation and virtual ethnography	—	Virtual ethnography of *SKAM* fans	Virtual ethnography of *SKAM* fans turned *blank* fans Observation of *blank* team
Document analysis	Institutional documents Press coverage	Institutional documents Press coverage	Institutional documents Press coverage Internal work documents
Audience ratings and statistics	Audience numbers and statistics	Audience numbers and statistics	Audience numbers and statistics Google Analytics

[6] Thanks to Kristian Tolonen, Håkon Lund Sørensen and Iacob Prebensen at NRK's division for audience insight for providing audience ratings regarding *Lilyhammer*, *SKAM* and *blank*. Thanks also to Kim Erlandsen, Tom Øverlie and Rashid Akrim at NRK P3 for their in-depth insights into Google Analytics and fan behaviour from an industry perspective.

THREE MEDIA STUDY TOPICS ACTIVATED BY TELEVISION STREAMING

This book analyses streaming through the lens of one particular public service broadcaster and some of its game-changing drama series. It relates, however, to profound topics within media studies, most importantly, issues related to national television, public service television and the end of television. Although none of these topics are new (rather the contrary!), they gain renewed importance in the current streaming context.

National Television

The first topic relates to the issue of *national television*. It marshals perspectives on globalisation, media flows and transnational television to engage with the effects of television streaming on national players and markets. Topics related to global media and globalisation—and the effect on national media—have occupied researchers for decades (Flew et al. 2016) but have renewed urgency as global (often US-based) platforms continue to take key positions in national markets (Cunningham and Silver 2013; Lobato 2019). On the one hand, global streaming services and digital portals—Netflix, YouTube, Facebook and so on—are seen to threaten established business models and the economic foundation of national media and potentially jeopardise national culture, identity, language and even democracy (Andrews 2019; Evens and Donders 2018). On the other hand, these providers facilitate opportunities for audiences in terms of access to content and services, and for national media players in terms of their reach regarding potential partners and markets. Furthermore, the process of globalisation is dynamic and complex, and global platforms can also adapt to national conditions. For instance, Ramon Lobato (2019) finds that there is no operative 'Netflix effect' on a global scale, noting instead that Netflix should be seen as 'a collection of national media services tied together in one platform rather than as a uniform global service' (2019: 182–184). Moreover, even if both US drama productions and streaming platforms have become hugely popular in large parts of the world, there have been continued demand for domestic services and products, and, in Europe, also willing to use public funding to sustain quality productions (see also Enli and Syvertsen 2016; Steemers 2004).

Studies of tensions between national and international interests and stakeholders are a favoured research object. For instance, questions about global 'media flows' can be traced back to the 1960s, when researchers started to theorise the existence of an unbalanced, indirect flow of information and media content from the 'center' to the 'periphery' (Schiller 1971). In one well-known study, Kaarle Nordenstreng and Tapio Varis (1974) describe television flow between nations as a 'one-way street' (1974: 52) within which US programmes, productions and distributions were assigned a particularly powerful role. Following this line of thought, scholars put forward the concept of 'cultural imperialism' while warning against 'cultural hegemony' and 'Americanisation' (Boyd-Barrett 1977).

From the 1980s onwards, the school of cultural studies brought a new strand of research into the debate by shifting the focus from 'the macro level of power relation between nations and corporations to content and the audience' (Iordache et al. 2019). Audience studies found that foreign media products were often subject to local reception processes through which the audience decoded media texts according to their unique knowledge and cultural background (Ang 1985; Liebes and Katz 1999). Studies also noted that audiences seemed to prefer content reflecting familiar cultural elements, which led to Joseph D. Straubhaar's (2007) notion of 'cultural proximity'. Scholars began to discuss two-way flows of content and focused on expressions of resistance from the 'periphery' by introducing terms such as 'counterflows' and 'contra-flows' (Thussu 2007)—Elke Weissmann's (2012) study of US and UK dramas, for example, locates a dynamic pattern of flow, counter-flow and sub-flow of content. Similar, Pia Majbritt Jensen (2016) used the term 'peripheral counter-flow' to describe the way in which successful Danish drama exports introduced an 'idea-based' and 'creative' counter-flow which impacted not only the language used in television series but also their forms of production, narrative themes and aesthetic characteristics (see also Redvall 2013). This notion of a creative counter-flow resonates well with studies of transnational film and television audiences which argue that the attraction of cultural products originating from elsewhere resides in perceived similarities *and* the experience of difference (Athique 2016; see also Jensen and Jacobsen 2020; Waade et al. 2020a). As explained by Michele Hilmes and her colleagues (2019), the term 'transnational' implies '"going beyond" the nation and the national in some ways, while still drawing on national identity for at least part of its coherence' (2019: 3).

Public Service Television

The second topic concerns *public service television*. While public service institutions and their cultural obligations and value schemes retain key positions in many Western European countries, the US television market has always been more liberalised and influenced by private and commercial companies and interests (Hallin and Mancini 2004; see also Brüggemann et al. 2014). Hence, the shift towards a globalised streaming market involves not only more international players but also more players driven by private and commercial interests. As a consequence, streaming increases the tension between public and private interest also in nations previously regulated through solid public service institutions (see also Freedman and Goblot 2018; Iosifidis 2010).

As with the previous topic, also studies of public service is a favoured research object. For instance, many studies have chartered the transition from public service *broadcasting* to public service *media* (Iosifidis 2007) as well as these institutions' expansion to digital media and 'new' platforms (Levy 1999; Moe 2009). Studies have also shown that public service institutions remain a significant force in many countries (Evens and Donders 2019) and continue to engage a broad range of stakeholder, despite the ongoing narrative of doom for legacy media (Sundet and Syvertsen 2020; Van den Bulck and Donders 2014). Furthermore, studies have shown that attempts to restrict public service on the European level have not been successful and that much of the future for public service institutions continues to be determined on a national level (Donders 2012). Naturally, then, studies also find different national policy makers and stakeholder to ascribe different roles to public service institutions in various cultural context (Tambini 2015).

In many Western European countries, public service institutions are seen as a cornerstone of the public sphere, and in countries such as the Nordic, they are also important welfare state institutions (Syvertsen et al. 2014: chapter 4). With their goals of universality and mixed programming and their serious obligations to develop and strengthen culture and democracy, public service institutions represent transformative and equalising institutions with great relevance to the cultural fabric. Several studies have also shown that public service institutions in these countries are well positioned to address the changing conditions and challenges of new-media contexts such as streaming (Syvertsen et al. 2014). Hanne Bruun describes them as 'adaptive, flexible and pragmatic' (2020: 15), both technologically and culturally.

The strong position of some public service institutions have not gone without dispute, however, and in the Nordic countries, they have been criticised for being *too* popular and successful in their expansion into streaming and new-media platforms (Sjøvaag et al. 2019; Sundet and Syvertsen 2020). While national television players (private and public) tend to agree that the competition with global streaming services is increasing, they do not agree on how to best secure national players or what role public service institutions should play (see also Nielsen et al. 2016; Sehl et al. 2020).

The End of Television

The third and last topic concerns the future of television, often termed as 'the end of television' in utopian and dystopian scenarios. The blurring of lines between different media sectors, the influx of global streaming services and digital intermediaries into national media markets, new user habits and changing business models have inspired many scholars to discuss changes in television, as a medium, industry, and political and cultural institution (Jenner 2018; Johnson 2018, 2019). While some frame these discussions as 'the end of television' (Katz and Scannell 2009; Spiegel and Olsson 2004), others talk of 'revolution' (Lotz 2007), 'reinvention' (Jenner 2018) and even a 'golden age' in creativity and programme production (Jenkins et al. 2013; McElroy and Noonan 2019). Scholars have also suggested separating television through different definitions—'post-network television', 'internet-distributed television', 'streaming television' and 'online TV' (see Johnson 2019 for a useful discussion, see also Lotz 2007, 2018). Despite attempts at clarification, however, it is not always easy to understand which aspects of television are changing or challenged by which forces. Furthermore, understandings of what television is and how it is changing are also fluctuated according to perspectives and stakeholder interests (Enli and Syvertsen 2016: 144).

Again, this topic is a favoured research object. Already in the 1970s, Raymond Williams (2005 [1974]) was writing about the 'invention of television' and how technology shape this shifting cultural medium. As Williams highlights, television was not defined from the start and the introduction of television caused a series of debates about how to characterise it (see also Ellis 2000; Fiske 2006 [1987]). Relatedly, Amanda D. Lotz (2007) discerns three eras in US television history—the network era (1950s–1980s), the transitional multi channel era (1980s–1990s) and the post-network era (2000 onwards)—and compares them to technology, creation, distribution, advertising and audience research. One insight is that 'new' distribution technology (whether VCR, DVD, TiVo, VOD or streaming) has invited more aggressive individual time management at the expense of network scheduling, with significant consequences for the industry. In later work, Lotz (2017, 2018) follows the accelerated evolution from cable television (HBO) to streaming services (Netflix), a rate of change which leads her to speak about 'the future of televisions' rather than the 'future of television' (Lotz 2020; see also Scannell 2020). As new modes of distribution arise, the industry adapts: change, as they say, is the only constant (see also Johnson 2019).

According to Gunn Enli and Trine Syvertsen (2016), at least three factors are essential in debates about the future of television that all have relevance for the scope of this book. To start with, end of television debates are often informed by a rhetoric of change put forward by actors who have a stake in the realisation of such predictions. One example is the CEO of Netflix, Reed Hastings, who several times has argued for 'the end of broadcast TV' (DTVE 2014; Seward 2015)—a scenario well-fitting for Netflix business model. Another example is HBO's well-known slogan, 'It's not TV. It's HBO'—aiming to signal HBO's distinctiveness compared to network television. Second, Enli and Syvertsen argue, the end of television debates often belittle the fact that technological change is meet with industry strategies and responses. Technology alone does not drive change, and national industry players are forces of change as well. As already described, several studies have pointed to national public service institutions as particular important 'locomotive' for experimentation and innovation, highlighting how changing conditions often leads these institutions to experiment and test new grounds (Bruun 2019; Evens and Donders 2018; Steemers 2004). Essential in these institutions' decision-making processes is how they perceive change, and a key topic for scholars should therefore be to detect how industry players identify opportunities and challenges, advantages and disadvantages, and benefits and risks. Third, and relatedly, Enli and Syvertsen argue that end of television discussions cannot be addressed adequately on a general level but needs to incorporate both local and contextual factors as well as strategic responses by existing television institutions within national contexts (see also Lobato 2019). Studies such as this one fit well with this call.

OUTLINE OF THE BOOK

A key argument of this book is that streaming impacts television drama in various ways ranging from how television executives think and talk about key industry shifts to the production of television drama, its publishing and contextualisation, and its new industry–audience relations. The analysis looks at why and how these changes are taking place and what implications they have. Many of the tendencies discussed do not come from streaming alone. For example, television executives develop new ways of producing and publishing television drama for a lot of reasons, not solely to meet the changes presented by streaming. I recognise that other driving forces exist, but focus this book on production models, publishing strategies and industry–audience relation developed in a streaming context. More specifically, I address how streaming provides both new *opportunities* and *challenges* for national players such as the NRK, and how NRK responds to make the most of the new situation. While the next four chapters discuss different aspects of television streaming, they all relate to perceived opportunities and challenges.

Chapter 2 discusses how television executives *envision* the industry changes which are taking place, arguing that streaming is understood to redefine the competitive landscape and transform the competition from national to international in scope. Several studies illustrate how 'industry lore' (Havens and Lotz 2012) and working notions guide industry decision-making in times of change, and this chapter aims to identify industry perceptions of television streaming and create a contextual framework for the more case-based analyses of the following chapters. The chapter is organised according to four key challenges: retaining the audience, creating 'world-class content', gaining visibility and securing content rights.

Chapter 3 discusses how streaming affects *television production*—that is, the way in which television drama is produced to accommodate a more on-demand and potentially more international audience through new forms of partnership, new production models and new storytelling techniques. The chapter is organised according to three particular drama production models favoured by streaming: 'going big', 'going small' and 'going again'. By analysing these models, the chapter demonstrates that television streaming has increased the need for high-budget 'world-class' drama series but also smaller, more niche-oriented (online) drama productions, as well as drama remakes and adaptations.

Chapter 4 discusses how streaming affects *television publishing*—that is, how online and on-demand television consumption contests the traditional publishing strategies of linear 'flow' television (Williams 2005 [1974]), and how the industry has responded by developing new ways to present, contextualise and distribute drama content. The chapter is organised according to three key publishing trends involving the reinvention of 'flow' and 'liveness', the creation of transmedia universes and, finally, events. By analysing these trends, the chapter demonstrates how the new television landscape increasingly blurs the lines between storytelling, distribution and promotion while adding additional layers of meaning for the audience to explore.

Chapter 5 discusses how streaming affects *industry–audience relations*—that is, the ways in which the industry perceives its viewers and tries to attract them, measure them and build loyal and engaging relationships with them. The chapter revisits the concept of 'audience making' (Ang 2005 [1991]) and looks at new opportunities for accommodating the audience in the move from linear to on-demand consumption models, as well as the value of measuring audience engagement and fan activity when gauging a show's success. The chapter is organised according to three ways streaming affect industry–audience relations: the way the industry perceives its audience, the ways the industry serves particular interested audiences—fans—and the ways the audiences are used by the industry to measure success.

The final chapter compares and contrasts aspects of television consumption through streaming in terms of its impact on television-related practice. It reframes streaming in terms of the three key topics: the redefinition of national television, television in the public interest and the end of television. Furthermore, it contests the claims that television is dying and that the 'love affair' between the industry and its audience has ended.

References

Andersen, Mads Møller. 2019. *DR og det creative pres.* PhD thesis, Aarhus University.
Andrews, Leighton. 2019. *Facebook, The Media and Democracy. Big Tech, Small State?* London and New York: Routledge.

Ang, Ien. 1985. *Watching Dallas: Soap Opera and the Melodramatic Imagination.* London: Routledge.

———. 2005 [1991]. *Desperately Seeking the Audience.* London and New York: Routledge.

Athique, Adrian. 2016. *Transnational Audiences. Media Reception on a Global Scale.* Cambridge: Polity.

Bakøy, Eva, Tore Helseth, and Roel Puijk, eds. 2016. *Bak kamera. Norsk film og TV i et produksjonsperspektiv.* Vallset: Oplandske Bokforlag.

Bakøy, Eva, Roel Puijk, and Andrew Spicer, eds. 2017. *Building Successful and Sustainable Film and Television Businesses: A Cross-national Perspective.* Bristol: Intellect.

Banks, Miranda J. 2014. How to Study Makers and Making. In *The SAGE Handbook of Television Studies,* eds. Manuel Alvarado, Milly Buonanno, Herman Gray, and Toby Miller, 117–132. London: Sage Publications.

Banks, Miranda, Bridget Conor, and Vicki Mayer, eds. 2015. *Production Studies, The Sequel! Cultural Studies of Global Media Industries.* London and New York: Routledge.

Baym, Nancy. 2000. *Tune In, Log On: Fandom and Online Community.* Thousand Oaks, CA: Sage Publications.

blank. 2018–2019. NRK.

Bore, Inger-Lise Kalviknes. 2017. *Screen Comedy and Online Audiences.* London: Routledge.

Boyd-Barrett, Oliver. 1977. Media Imperialism: Towards an International Framework for an Analysis of Media Systems. *Mass Communication and Society.* 116–135.

Brüggemann, Michael, Sven Engesser, Florin Büchel, Edda Humprecht, and Laia Castro. 2014. Hallin and Mancini Revisited: Four Empirical Types of Western Media Systems. *Journal of Communication* 64 (6): 1037–1065.

Bruun, Hanne. 2016. The Qualitative Interview in Media Production Studies. In *Advancing Media Production Research: Shifting Sites, Methods, and Politics,* eds. Chris Paterson, David Lee, Anamik Saha, and Anna Zoellner, 131–146. London: Palgrave Macmillan.

———. 2020. *Re-Scheduling Television in the Digital Era.* London and New York: Routledge.

Caldwell, John T. 2008. *Production Culture. Industrial Reflexivity and Critical Practice in Film and Television.* London: Duke University Press.

———. 2009. Cultures of Production: Studying Industry's Deep Texts, Reflexive Rituals and Managed Self-Disclosures. In *Media Industries: History, Theory, and Method,* eds. Jennifer Holt and Alisa Perren, 199–212. West Sussex: Wiley-Blackwell.

Carlström, Wilhelm. 2017. Six Countries Set for Remakes of Norway's Hit Show Skam – And the American Version Will Air on Facebook's Watch Service. *Nordic Business Insider*, October 18.

Carr, Austin. 2012. Traditional TV, Get You "Hooked" On All-At-Once Watching. *Fast Company*, July 2.

Cavicchi, Daniel. 1998. *Tramps Like Us: Music and Meaning Among Springsteen Fans*. New York: Oxford University Press.

Creeber, Glen. 2015. Killing Us Softly: Investigating the Aesthetics, Philosophy and Influence of Nordic Noir Television. *The Journal of Popular Television* 3 (1): 21–35.

Cunningham, Stuart, and Jon Silver. 2013. *Screen Distribution and the New King Kongs of the Online World*. New York: Palgrave Pivot.

Donadio, Rachel. 2016. Will 'Skam', a Norwegian Hit, Translate? *New York Times*, December 9.

Donders, Karen. 2012. *Public Service Media and Policy in Europe*. London: Palgrave.

DTVE. 2014. Netflix Boss Predicts the End of Broadcast TV. *Digital TV Europe*, November 28.

Duffett, Mark. 2017. *Understanding Fandom. An Introduction to the Study of Media Fan Culture*. New York: Bloomsbury.

Ellis, John. 2000. *Seeing Things. Television in the Age of Uncertainty*. London and New York: I. B. Tauris Publishing.

Enli, Gunn, and Trine Syvertsen. 2016. The End of Television—Again! How TV Is Still Influenced by Cultural Factors in the Age of Digital Intermediaries. *Media and Communication* 4 (3): 142–153.

Evans, Elizabeth. 2011. *Transmedia Television*. New York: Routledge.

———. 2020. *Understanding Engagement in Transmedia Culture*. London and New York: Routledge.

Evens, Tom, and Karen Donders. 2018. *Platform Power and Policy in Transforming Television Markets*. Cham, Switzerland: Palgrave Macmillan.

Faldalen, Jon Inge. 2016. -Nerven i 'Skam' skal være sterk og relevant. Rushprint. no, 4 April.

Fiske, John. 2006 [1987]. *Television Culture*. London and New York: Routledge.

Flew, Terry, Petros Iosifidis, and Jeanette Steemers, eds. 2016. *Global Media and National Policies*. London: Palgrave Macmillan.

Fordal, Jo Annar. 2015. A Gigantic Small Broadcaster. *NRK.no*, June 26.

Freedman, Des, and Vana Goblot, eds. 2018. *A Future for Public Service Television*. London: Goldsmiths Press.

Geertz, Clifford. 1973. *The Interpretation of Cultures*. New York: Basic Books.

Gray, Jonathan. 2010. *Show Sold Separately. Promos, Spoilers, and Other Media Paratexts*. New York: New York University Press.

Gray, Jonathan, and Amanda D. Lotz. 2012. *Television Studies*. Cambridge: Polity Press.

Hallin, Daniel C., and Paolo Mancini. 2004. *Comparing Media Systems: Three Models of Media and Politics*. Cambridge: Cambridge University Press.

Hansen, Magne. 2013. Lilyhammer solgt til over 139 land. *NRK.no*, 15 February.

Hansen, Kim Tofte, and Anne Marit Waade. 2017. *Locating Nordic Noir. From Beck to The Bridge*. Hampshire: Palgrave Macmillan.

Harrington, C. Lee, and Denis D. Bielby. 1995. *Soap Fans. Pursuing Pleasure and Making Meaning in Everyday Life*. Philadelphia: Temple University Press.

Havens, Timothy, and Amanda D. Lotz. 2012. *Understanding Media Industries*. New York: Oxford University Press.

Havens, Timothy, Amanda D. Lotz, and Serra Tinic. 2009. Critical Media Industry Studies: A Research Approach. *Communication, Culture & Critique* 2: 234–253.

Herbert, Daniel, Amanda D. Lotz, and Aswin Punathambekar. 2020. *Media Industry Studies*. Cambridge: Polity.

Hertz, Roseanna, and Jonathan Imber, eds. 1995. *Studying Elites Using Qualitative Methods*. Thousand Oaks: Sage Publications.

Hill, Annette. 2019. *Media Experiences. Engaging with Drama and Reality Television*. London and New York: Routledge.

Hills, Matt. 2002. *Fan Cultures*. London and New York: Routledge.

Hills, Matt, Michele Hilmes, and Roberta Pearson, eds. 2019. *Transatlantic Television Drama. Industries, Programmes, & Fans*. Oxford: Oxford University Press.

Holmes, Michele, Roberta Pearson, and Matt Hills. 2019. Flying the Flag for Contemporary Transatlantic Television Drama. In *Transatlantic Television Drama. Industries, Programmes, & Fans*, eds. Matt Hills, Michele Hilmes, and Roberta Pearson, 1–23. Oxford: Oxford University Press.

Holt, Jennifer, and Alisa Perren, eds. 2009. *Media Industries. History, Theory, and Method*. Oxford: Wiley-Blackwell.

Holt, Jennifer, and Kevin Sanson, eds. 2014. *Connected Viewing. Selling, Streaming, & Sharing Media in the Digital Era*. London: Routledge.

Iordache, Catalina, Leo Van Audenhove, and Jan Loisen. 2019. Global Media Flows: A Qualitative Review of Research Methods in Audio-Visual Flow Studies. *The International Communication Gazette* 81 (6–7–8): 748–767.

Iosifidis, Petros. 2007. *Public Television in the Digital Era Technological Challenges and New Strategies for Europe*. Basingstoke: Palgrave.

———, ed. 2010. *Reinventing Public Service Communication. European Broadcasters and Beyond*. London: Palgrave Macmillan.

Jenkins, Henry. 1992. *Textual Poachers. Television Fans & Participatory Culture*. New York: Routledge.

———. 2006. *Convergence Culture. Where Old and New Media Collide.* New York and London: New York University Press.

———. 2016. Fan studies. *Oxford Bibliographies.*

Jenkins, Henry, Sam Ford, and Joshua Green. 2013. *Spreadable Media. Creating Value and Meaning in a Networked Culture.* New York: New York University Press.

Jenner, Mareike. 2018. *Netflix and the Re-Invention of Television.* London: Palgrave Macmillan.

Jensen, Jolie. 1992. Fandom as Pathology: The Consequences of Characterization. In *The Adoring Audience. Fan Culture and Popular Media*, ed. Lisa A. Lewis, 9–29. London & New York: Routledge.

Jensen, Pia Majbritt. 2016. Global Impact of Danish Drama Series: A Peripheral, Non-Commercial Creative Counter-Flow. *Kosmorama* #263.

Jensen, Pia Majbritt, and Ushma Chauhan Jacobsen, eds. 2020. *The Global Audiences of Danish Television Drama.* Göteborg: Nordicom.

Johnson, Derek, ed. 2018. *From Networks to Netflix. A Guide to Changing Channels.* London: Routledge.

Johnson, Catherine. 2019. *Online TV.* London and New York: Routledge.

Kampanje. 2019. Norsk drama-boom til over 600 millioner kroner: – Her er årets mest sette dramaserier. *Kampanje.com*, May 11.

Kantar. 2016. Kantar Unveils the World's Most Advanced Hybrid Model in Norway to Deliver Total TV & Video Currency. *Kantarmedia.com*, August 25.

Katz, Elihu and Paddy Scannell, eds. 2009. The End of Television? Its Impact on the World (So Far). Special Issue in *The Annuals of the American Academy of Political and Social Science* 625.

Klebnikov, Sergei. 2020. Streaming Wars Continue: Here's How Much Netflix, Amazon, Disney+ and Their Rivals Are Spending on New Content. *Forbes*, May 22.

Levine, Elena. 2001. Towards a Paradigm for Media Production Research: Behind the Scenes at the General Hospital. *Critical Studies in Media Communication* 18 (1): 66–82.

Levy, David. 1999. *Europe's Digital Revolution: Broadcasting Regulation, the EU and the Nation State.* London and New York: Routledge.

Liebes, Tamar, and Elihu Katz. 1999. *The Export of Meaning: Cross-Cultural Readings of Dallas.* Cambridge: Oxford University Press.

Lilyhammer. 2012–2014. Rubicon TV for NRK and Netflix.

Littleton, Cynthia, and Elaine Low. 2019. Adapt or Die: Why 2020 Will Be All About Entertainment's New Streaming Battleground. *Variety*, December 17.

Lobato, Ramon. 2019. *Netflix Nations. The Geography of Digital Distribution.* New York: New York University Press.

Lotz, Amanda D. 2007. *The Television Will Be Revolutionized.* New York: New York University Press.

———. 2017. *Portals: A Treatise on Internet-Distributed Television*. Michigan Publishing.

———. 2018. *We Now Disrupt This Broadcast. How Cable Transformed Television and the Internet Revolutionized It All*. Cambridge: The MIT Press.

———. 2020. The Future of Televisions, a Response. *Media, Culture & Society* 42 (5): 800–802.

Lüders, Marika. 2007. *Being in Mediated Spaces. An Enquiry into Personal Media Practices*. PhD thesis, University of Oslo.

Mayer, Vicki, Miranda J. Banks, and John T. Caldwell. 2009a. Introduction. Production Studies: Roots and Routes. In *Production Studies. Cultural Studies of Media Industries*, eds. Vicki Mayer, Miranda J. Banks, and John T. Caldwell, 1–12. London: Routledge.

Mayer, Vicki, Miranda J. Banks, and John Thornton Caldwell, eds. 2009b. *Production Studies. Cultural Studies of Media Industries*. New York: Routledge.

McElroy, Ruth, and Caitriona Noonan. 2019. *Producing British Television Drama. Local Production in a Global Era*. London: Palgrave Macmillan.

Meld. St. 28. 2014–2015. *Open og opplyst. Allmennkringkasting og mediemangfold*.

Moe, Hallvard. 2009. *Public Broadcasting, the Internet and Democracy. Comparing Policy and Exploring Public Service Media Online*. PhD thesis, University of Bergen.

Nielsen, Rasmus Kleis, Richard Fletcher, Annika Sehl, and David Levy. 2016. *Analysis of the Relation Between and Impact of Public Service Media and Private Media*. Oxford: Reuters Institute for Study of Journalism (RISJ).

Nordenstreng, Kaarle, and Tapio Varis. 1974. *Television Traffic – A One Way Street? A Survey and Analysis of the International Flow of Television Programme Material*. Reports and Papers on Mass Communication No. 70. Paris: UNESCO.

NRK. 2019. *Liste over eksterne produksjoner*. Oslo: NRK.

———. 2020. *NRKs årsrapport 2019*. Oslo: NRK.

Paterson, Chris, David Lee, Anamik Saha, and Anna Zoellner, eds. 2016. *Advancing Media Production Research: Shifting Sites, Methods, and Politics*. London: Palgrave Macmillan.

Pertierra, Anna Cristina, and Graeme Turner. 2013. *Locating Television: Zones of Consumption*. London and New York: Routledge.

Petersen, Line Nybro, and Vilde Schanke Sundet. 2019. Play Moods Across the Life Course in *SKAM* Fandom. *Journal of Fandom Studies* 7 (2): 113–131.

Pink, Sarah, Heather Horst, John Postill, Larissa Hjorth, Tania Lewis, and Jo Tacchi. 2016. *Digital Ethnography. Principles and Practice*. London: Sage Publishing.

Redvall, Eva Novrup. 2013. *Writing and Producing Television Drama in Denmark: From the Kingdom to the Killing*. Hampshire: Palgrave Macmillan.

Sandvik, Ingvar, Alexadra Kanutte-Skåre, and Jonas Østnes. 2020. *Generasjoner. Fra Gen Z til Boomers*. Oslo: Kantar.

Sandvoss, Cornel. 2005. *Fans: The Mirror of Consumption*. Cambridge: Polity Press.

Scannell, Paddy. 2020. The Future of Television. *Media, Culture & Society* 42 (2). 293–300.

Schiller, Herbert I. 1971. *Mass Communication and American Empire*. Boston, MA: Beacon Press.

Sehl, Annika, Richard Fletcher, and Robert G. Picard. 2020. Crowding Out: Is There Evidence That Public Service Media Harm Markets? A Cross-National Comparative Analysis of Commercial Television and Online News Providers. *European Journal of Communication* 35 (4): 389–409.

Sepinwall, Alan. 2020. Who Loses Big in the Great Streaming Wars? The User. *The Rolling Stones*, July 23.

Seward, Zachary M. 2015. Netflix's Reed Hastings Predicts the Future of TV over the Next 20 Years. *Quartz*, May 11.

Shaw, Lucas. 2019. What the Streaming War Mean for the Future of Television. *Bloomberg*, November 20.

Sjøvaag, Helle, Truls Andre Pedersen, and Thomas Owren. 2019. Is Public Service Broadcasting a Threat to Commercial Media. *Media, Culture & Society* 41 (6): 808–827.

SKAM/SHAME. 2015–2017. NRK.

Spiegel, Lynn, and Jahn Olsson, eds. 2004. *Television After TV: Essays on a Medium in Transition*. Durham: Duke University Press.

SSB. 2020. *Norsk Mediebarometer 2019*. Oslo: SSB.

Steemers, Jeanette. 2004. *Selling Television. British Television in the Global Marketplace*. London: British Film Institute.

———. 2016. International Sales of U.K. Television Content: Change and Continuity in "the Space Between" Production and Consumption. *Television & New Media* 17 (8): 734–753.

Stein, Louisa Ellen. 2015. *Millennial Fandom: Television Audiences in the Transmedia Age*. Iowa City: University of Iowa Press.

Stokel-Walker, Chris. 2017. *Skam*: How a Web-Based Norwegian Teen Drama Is Changing How We Watch TV. *The Telegraph*, December 5.

Straubhaar, Joseph D. 2007. *World Television: From Global to Local*. Los Angeles: Sage Publication.

Strømmen, Nils Petter. 2020. Medietrender Ung 12–19. Oslo: Kantar.

Sundet, Vilde Schanke. 2016. Still 'Desperately Seeking the Audience'? Audience Making in the Age of Media Convergence (the *Lilyhammer* Experience). *Northern Lights* 14 (1): 11–27.

———. 2017a. Co-produced Television and the Cost of Transnational 'Success': The Making of *Lilyhammer*. In *Building Successful and Sustainable Film and Television Businesses: A Cross-national Perspective*, eds. Eva Bakøy, Roel Puijk, and Andrew Spicer, 67–88. Bristol: Intellect.

———. 2017b. 'Det er bare du som kan føle det du føler' – emosjonell investering og engasjement i nettdramaet *SKAM. 16:9 Filmtidsskrift.*

———. 2019. From Secret Online Teen Drama to International Cult Phenomenon: The Global Expansion of *SKAM* and Its Public Service Mission. *Critical Studies in Television* 15 (1): 69–90.

———. 2020. Drama as Flagship Productions: Small Nations Television and Digital Distribution. In *Danish Television Drama: Global Lessons from a Small Nation*, eds. Anne Marit Waade, Eva Novrup Redvall, and Pia Majbritt Jensen, 147–165. Palgrave Macmillan.

Sundet, Vilde Schanke, and Line Nybro Petersen. 2020. Ins and Outs of Transmedia Fandom: Motives for Entering and Exiting the *SKAM* Fan Community Online. *Poetics.* Online First. https://doi.org/10.1016/j. poetic.2020.101510.

Sundet, Vilde Schanke, and Trine Syvertsen. 2020. From Problem to Solution? Why It Is Difficult to Restrict the Remit of Public Broadcasters. *International Journal of Cultural Policy.* Online First. https://doi.org/10.1080/1028663 2.2020.1807522.

Syvertsen, Trine. 1997. *Den store tv-krigen. Norsk allmennfjernsyn 1988–96.* Bergen: Fagbokforlaget.

———. 2004. Citizens, Audiences, Consumers and Players: A Conceptual Discussion of the Relationship Between Broadcasters and Their Publics. *European Journal of Cultural Studies* 7 (3): 363–380.

Syvertsen, Trine, Gunn Enli, Ole J. Mjøs, and Hallvard Moe. 2014. *The Media Welfare State: Nordic Media in the Digital Era.* Ann Arbor: University of Michigan Press.

Tambini, Damian. 2015. Problems and Solutions for Public Service Broadcasting: Reflections on a 56 Country Study. In *Public Service Media in Europe: A Comparative Approach*, eds. Karen Arriaza Ibarra, Eva Nowak, and Raymond Kuhn, 41–52. London: Routledge

Te Walvaart, Maarlene. 2020. *Engaging the Audience. Production Perspectives in Current Affairs Television.* PhD dissertation, University of Antwerp.

Thussu, Daya Kishan, ed. 2007. *Media on the Move Global Flow and Contra-Flow.* New York: Routledge.

Van den Bulck, Hilde, and Karen Donders. 2014. Of Discourses, Stakeholders and Advocacy Coalitions in Media Policy: Tracing Negotiations Towards the New Management Contract of Flemish Public Broadcaster VRT. *European Journal of Communication* 29 (1): 83–99.

Waade, Anne Marit, Eva Novrup Redvall, and Pia Majbritt Jensen. 2020a. Transnational Television Drama? Lessons Learned from Danish Drama. In *Danish Television Drama. Global Lessons from a Small Nation*, eds. Anne Marit Waade, Eva Novrup Redvall, and Pia Majbritt Jensen, 1–22. London: Palgrave Macmillan.

————, eds. 2020b. *Danish Television Drama. Global Lessons from a Small Nation.* London: Palgrave Macmillan.

Wallace, Petter. 2015. Head of External Productions at NRK. In-Person interview, Oslo, January 15.

Weissmann, Elke. 2012. *Transnational Television Drama: Special Relations and Mutual Influence Between the US and UK.* New York: Palgrave Macmillan.

Williams, Raymond. 2005 [1974]. *Television: Technology and Cultural Form.* London: Routledge.

Williams, Rebecca. 2015. *Post-Object Fandom. Television, Identify and Self-Narrative.* New York: Bloomsbury.

CHAPTER 2

Industry Perceptions of Streaming

Abstract Several studies illustrate the ways in which *industry perceptions* guide decision-making in times of change and advocate for the importance of identifying such notions. This chapter uncovers key perceptions of television streaming and addresses, in particular, how television executives envision the impact of streaming when making drama shows. It finds that streaming is thought to redefine the competitive landscape while transforming it from national to international in scope. It also identifies four related challenges: *retaining the audience* in an increasingly globalised television landscape, *creating 'world-class content'* to compete with internationally oriented productions, *gaining visibility* amid an abundance of high-quality series and *securing long-term and flexible content rights* when the conditions become a 'global battlefield'.

Keywords Industry perceptions • Public service broadcasting • Streaming • Television drama • Television studies • World-class content

INTRODUCTION

How do industry decision-makers *envision* the impact of television streaming on the production and publishing of television drama, and what do they perceive to be the main opportunities and challenges in this regard? This chapter aims to identify key *industry perceptions* of television streaming, based on the assumption that such industry notions are important to

V. S. Sundet, *Television Drama in the Age of Streaming*,
https://doi.org/10.1007/978-3-030-66418-3_2

study because they describe 'common-sense ideas' (Havens and Lotz 2012: 137) which inform industry strategies and practices and link industry beliefs to industry interests (Sundet and Ytreberg 2009). Decision-makers often regard industry notions as 'truths' rather than ideas or perceptions, but their ultimate truthfulness is not as important as their impact upon strategic decisions and practices—that is, how they guide action in times of uncertainty. That said, industry perceptions also clearly have strategic consequences, meaning that the way executives *want* to see things often influences the way they respond. It is this dynamic which particularly engages the critical attention of scholars.

In order to map industry perceptions of television streaming, this chapter builds on interviews with numerous NRK executives. It pays particular interest to the ways top-level management defines the overall changes taking place and the actions NRK should take to meet them.[1] These executives by no means represent all relevant perspectives on streaming in a big organisation like NRK, but their thinking is of particular interest when one is trying to identify how NRK addresses change on a *strategic* level, as well as how these strategies are translated into actions and practices. In the more detailed case studies which follow this chapter (see Chaps. 3, 4 and 5), perspectives from creative and more hands-on informants demonstrate that television streaming impacts all levels of NRK as an organisation, albeit in different ways and to different extents.

FROM NATIONAL COMPETITION TO WORLD CHAMPIONSHIP

One of the key findings from reviewing industry perceptions of television streaming is the notion that streaming fundamentally changes the 'rules of the game', forcing national media players to adapt to, in particular, its international competitors. Streaming is seen to represent a new era for the

[1] This group of informants includes NRK's Broadcasting Director (Thor Gjermund Eriksen, interviewed 2019), NRK's Head of Drama (Ivar Køhn, interviewed 2017), NRK's Head of Programme (Vibeke Fürst Haugen, interviewed 2015), NRK's Head of Media (Øyvind Lund, interviewed 2015), NRK's Head of Television (Arne Helsingen, interviewed 2015), NRK's Head of External Productions (Petter Wallace, interviewed 2015), NRK's Head of Analysis (Kristian Tolonen, interviewed 2015), NRK's Head of the TV Player (Nicolai Flesjø, interviewed 2015), NRK's Head of Super (Hildri Gulliksen, interviewed 2017) and NRK's Head of P3 (Camilla Bjørn, interviewed 2018). All the informants were interviewed at some point between 2015 and 2019, and their statements naturally reflect the time of their interviews (see more Chap. 1).

television industry—a 'game changer' with multiple structural consequences for everyone involved. One fundamental consequence is linked to
the notion that streaming crosses territorial boundaries and creates a more
globally oriented television market (see also Lobato 2019). For instance,
many informants said that the international (but US-based) streaming services like Netflix and HBO—and, later, Amazon Prime and Disney Plus—
change their television market from a 'national competition to a world
championship' (Eriksen interviewed 2019). Such a change represents a
real opportunity for independent producers looking for new (international) partners and for consumers looking for more drama series to watch.
It proves, however, troublesome for a small national broadcaster such as
NRK, which has long enjoyed a privileged public service broadcaster position and, thanks to national regulations, limited competition. NRK's
Head of Media stressed, 'I think the biggest change ahead is the fact that
technology has broken down territorial boundaries. We are now competing with *everyone*' (Lund interviewed 2015). In short, streaming is perceived to put pressure on NRK (and others) to make excellent content
which can 'compete with the best content from around the world, at all
times' (NRK 2014: 3). Streaming also facilitates the distribution of audio-
visual content on social media platforms such as YouTube, Instagram and
Facebook, thus crowding the marketplace even more. While these platforms often favour a different type of content (for instance, shorter formats and user-generated clips), they are nevertheless competing for the
audience's time and attention (see also Webster 2014). In short, during
my ten-year analysis period (2010–2019), NRK, in the eyes of the informants, had gone from a relatively protected existence to an existence
exposed to almost unlimited competition.

But what is involved in this new 'world championship of streaming',
exactly? Below, I will point to four challenges the informants perceived
had been brought by streaming to the making of television drama: *retaining the audience, creating world-class content, gaining visibility* and, finally,
securing content rights. These challenges are not unique to NRK and
appear as well in other studies of streaming's impact on national television
players and markets (see, for instance, Bruun 2020; Evens and Donders
2018; Johnson 2019; Lobato 2019; Lotz 2017; McElroy and Noonan
2019). They were, however, thought to gain momentum, demonstrating
how industry executives often need to develop strategies on moving
targets.

CHALLENGE 1: RETAINING THE AUDIENCE

Many informants stressed that streaming makes it harder to *retain the audience*, reflecting notions of an increasingly 'nomadic audience' (Silverstone 1999). As mentioned, streaming is seen to foster new relationships with the audience, undermining its existing 'love affair' with the NRK (Wallace interviewed 2015) and demanding new drama strategies as a result. The problem is not only that the audience now has more content to consume—and from a greater variety of (international) players—but also that the old scheduling strategies are less effective, forcing NRK (and others) to adopt new strategies for attracting, moving and keeping the audience (see also Bruun 2020; Jenner 2018). As such, many informants reflected a shift in the traditional push–pull dynamic (Hill 2019) between producers and audiences.

The challenge of retaining the audience is high on all the informants' agendas because NRK, a public service broadcaster, felt as beholden to a large and satisfied audience as any private or commercial television provider (see also Napoli 2011). NRK's Head of Media insisted, 'We are here for our audience, and our business models are based on an audience that finds it worthwhile to have a public service broadcaster' (Lund interviewed 2015). As many informants highlighted, a public broadcaster without a public risked losing the legitimacy it needs to survive. Besides, in the eyes of the informants, high-quality and important public service content has little value until it is consumed by the audience. There is no point without an audience.

The challenge of retaining the audience is perceived to impact both scheduling techniques and content strategies, thus affecting the whole organisation in strategic, creative, and more hands-on and practical ways. At the heart of this challenge is the notion that streaming—and the on-demand user mode it enabled—forces NRK to prioritise content which is 'choosable' (Bjørn interviewed 2018) and which will prompt the audience to choose NRK 'not only once, but again and again, all the time' (Køhn interviewed 2017). As a result, a general industry perception within NRK is that streaming undermines the ritual of watching flow television and make viewing, and particularly the process of deciding what to watch, a more conscious and deliberate act—one where the power of choice is increasingly in the hands of the audience rather than the broadcaster. Needless to say, this shift is seismic to NRK, as it is for any other broadcaster rooted in a scheduled world (see also Chap. 4). Moreover, the new emphasis on 'choosable content' is perceived to directly impact how NRK will go about fulfilling its core public service remit of providing a broad mix of content categories. Whereas NRK had long provided its audience with less popular content categories through various scheduling techniques and tent-poling strategies—'popular content lifts niche content', NRK's Broadcasting Director said (Eriksen 2015; see also Ihlebæk et al. 2014)—streaming requires new strategies for introducing the audience to less popular content, that is, to fulfil NRK's public service remit (see also Bruun 2020; Van den Bulck and Moe 2017). This notion, then, sees the audience as active, rational and in some sense thrifty in its deliberate search for high-quality content. It does not account for the difficulties many viewers face in choosing or even finding good content, or for the fact that audience behaviour is not always either rational or 'goal-oriented' (Webster 2014).

According to the informants, at least two types of strategies help the cause of retaining the audience during competition in the new 'world championship of streaming', above and beyond the obvious strategy of making high-quality content (to which I will return below). To start with, many emphasised the *need for relevance*—that is, that television drama now has to 'fill a need among the audience, instead of filling a need within the schedule' (Køhn interviewed 2017; see also Chap. 3). Hence, as established scheduling strategies lost their value, the executives decided to adjust the type of content being produced in the first place. Informants described the work involved in getting to know the audience better and capitalising upon available audience data when developing and producing television drama, and they noted that this work informed not only publishing strategies but also content production. As such, these informants were implying that 'audience making' (Ang 2005 [1991]; Ettema and Whitney 1994) holds more value than ever as globalisation continues to increase the competitiveness of the market (see also Chap. 5). NRK's Head of Programme explained, 'We need to do more audience research, and we need to use the audience more actively than we used to' (Haugen interviewed 2015). This strategy represents both a practical and a conceptual shift for the NRK, as it did for its peers (Ellis 2000; Ihlebæk et al. 2014).

Audience insight is far from a new priority at NRK, which has had a division devoted to analysing audience numbers since such measurements were systematically introduced in Norway in the early 1990s. Over time, however, this work has been given higher priority across more and more of NRK's organisation, and for top-level management, at least, knowledge about the audience is perceived to be 'essential' (Tolonen interviewed 2015). Many informants described an organisational shift towards an interest in audience insight and user data at NRK across the ten-year analysis period (Haugen interviewed 2015; Lund interviewed 2015; Køhn interviewed 2017).

The broadcaster also increasingly turned to new development tools such as the Needs, Approach, Benefits and Competition (NABC) model and the design-thinking approach to identify audience needs and build strategic and creative processes around them (Hedemann 2018: chapter 4). Following the NABC protocol, NRK staff conducted in-depth user interviews with representatives from the target audience to identify needs which then informed the subsequent content-development process. The aim was to make every project 'tailor-made' for its intended audience segment (Haugen interviewed 2015; see also Hedemann 2018: chapter 4; Redvall 2018). As NRK's Head of International Formats pointed out, 'many media companies have allowed their employees to cultivate what *they* find interesting rather than asking them to address the needs and problems of their audiences. (…) The NABC model forces us to focus on audience needs when developing new content' (Hedemann 2014: 35, 34, my translation). As we will see in the following chapter, this model—and NRK's general focus on audience needs—was one of the key aspects of both *SKAM* and *blank*.

In addition to highlighting the importance of relevance in terms of retaining the audience, many informants spoke strongly about the *need for shared experiences*, insisting that television—even in the age of streaming—had much to gain from creating shared arenas of experience and larger events (see also Chap. 4). NRK's Head of Media noted, 'People have a need to gather together. (…) They watch television not only because it is fun but also to create a common set of references' (Lund interviewed 2015). NRK's Head of Audience Insight agreed, 'People want to watch when everyone else is watching. The ritual of watching television together still stands strong' (Tolonen interviewed 2015). As such, many informants emphasised the role of television in creating 'imagined communities' (Anderson 1991 [1983]) and the value of the shared experience from the audience's perspective. Most members will never meet, yet they still share the image of their communion. A grander emphasis on television as a nation builder is even evident in NRK's ambitious slogan: 'NRK gathers the people' (NRK 2016: 2). The informants pointed to television drama as a particularly useful genre in this respect along with sports and 'event programmes' such as *Eurovision Song Contest* (see also Kjus 2009). Hence, while the personalised and on-demand user modes of streaming appear to challenge the social ritual of television viewing (Lull 1990), many informants pointed to collectiveness and 'eventification' as a way to reunify viewers. Attractive strategies for retaining the audience thus ranged from niche-oriented drama series based on specific audience needs to powerful and broad-based drama series which can unite the nation in common interest (see also Chap. 3).

Challenge 2: Producing World-Class Content

Next, and relatedly, many informants stressed the way in which streaming put pressure on NRK to *produce 'world-class content'*. Even as the explosion of new platforms and streaming services made the audience increasingly 'unfaithful' (Wallace interviewed 2015), the audience was also perceived to be more concerned with quality and less willing to spend time and energy on 'mediocre content', as one informant put it, 'While mediocre content can survive in a flow world, that is not the case in a streaming world' (Lund interviewed 2015). Many informants shared this view. Another added, 'We talk a lot about new platforms, flow, and non-flow, but it is really all about quality. (...) There is a direct relationship between quality—which, of course, is a flexible concept—and popularity and viewing numbers' (Wallace interviewed 2015). In short, streaming is perceived to increase audience expectations for television drama, which demanded, in turn, higher budgets and production values. Furthermore, many stressed that even important content needs to be presented in an entertaining fashion while still being of high quality. NRK's Broadcasting Director noted, 'Nothing is so important that it does not have to be top notch' (Eriksen interviewed 2019). This notion is also reflected in NRK's overall ambition to 'make the important popular and the popular important', which was introduced in NRK's long-term strategy for 2016 to 2021 (NRK 2016: 5).

High-quality content has always been valued in the television industry, especially when it comes to drama (McCabe and Akass 2007). Still, many informants describe a situation in which streaming is *increasing the audience's expectations regarding quality*, thus raising the bar for success. For one thing, they thought that streaming—and the overall industry focus on television drama—had educated the audience and made it more advanced, and to some degree also more exclusive, in its taste. Whereas the drama audiences in a linear 'flow world' were thought to be more accepting of various types of drama series if they were scheduled in a popular timeslot, the streaming audience was thought to be more deliberate and purposeful in their search for content. As such, many informants aligned with a notion in which the explosion of available drama content—and the concomitant freedom of choice—has taught the audience to seek out the very best. More indirectly, they evoked 'blockbuster' (Elberse 2013) and 'winner-take-all' (Frank and Coock 1995) logics, meaning that, first, the audience would choose the best available drama series at the time, not the second-best, and second, people—because they are inherently social—see value in consuming the same content as others, which again reinforces the popularity of some drama series over others (see also Frank and Coock 1995). NRK's Broadcasting Director argued:

> We now see a situation where the difference between a drama series that is really good and absolutely fantastic good makes all the difference in the world when it comes to becoming a success or a failure. It is almost binary: either it will be a success or it will go to hell. (Thor Gjermund Eriksen, NRK's Broadcasting Director, interviewed 2019)

Another way streaming is raising the bar for quality, many informants emphasised, is that its globalised market also means globalised production budgets—NRK is competing not only with 'everyone' (Lund interviewed 2015) but also with players with very deep pockets. A key perception among the informants, then, is that the demand for 'world-class content' quickly turns into a demand for 'world-class budgets'. For a small nation's public service broadcaster such as NRK, this was problematic as it has a hard time competing against bigger competitors aiming at larger, transnational markets. Economic analysis often claims that the revenue potential influences the programme's budget, linking quality with the budget invested in a production (Jayakar and Waterman 2000). Relatedly, Gillian Doyle (2016) describes how streaming services use high budget—'big statement drama'—to strengthen brands and attract subscribers. During the ten-year analysis period, NRK reallocated parts of its budget to strengthening its drama productions (Køhn interviewed 2017) and repeatedly reported breaking budget records on those projects (Michalsen 2017; Hauger 2019). Even so, NRK's drama budgets are nowhere near those of the international streaming services (Hayes 2020). NRK's Broadcasting Director compared Netflix's *The Crown*, 'which costs 1.3–1.2 billion

NOK each episode', to NRK's *State of Happiness* (*Lykkeland*), 'which costs 80 million NOK per season—that is, half of one episode of *The Crown*', to make his point: 'For our audiences, the quality expectation is the same, which means we have to find other ways of giving them unique quality' (Eriksen interviewed 2019). While the definition of 'unique quality' might vary, relevance is often perceived as a key selling point. Whereas international streaming services have access to seemingly unlimited budgets, NRK has a 'unique knowledge of Norwegian culture' (Gulliksen interviewed 2017), and precisely, local familiarity and relevance are considered key advantages in a globalised market, expressing the informants' belief in the power of 'cultural proximity' (Straubhaar 2007). Local familiarity is perceived to be a big part of both *Lilyhammer*'s and *SKAM*'s success in the national *and* international markets, as I will discuss further in the next chapter.

As many informants assured, the increased competition is not only a challenge but also an opportunity to 'step up', reprioritise and be more focused in ordering, commissioning and producing drama series. For instance, NRK's Head of Drama highlighted the need to rethink NRK's role as a drama producer in the new-media landscape: 'It makes us more focused in picking the right types of project and makes us rethink our role in the media system' (Køhn interviewed 2017). In short, aiming to be a 'world-class' drama producer meant choosing which battles to fight. It also meant looking for new and more cost-effective ways of producing drama content, both to create a surplus of options on the NRK player and to respond to the needs of particular niches, among them the youth. The call for 'world-class' content thus encompassed various production models accommodating both series which sought to create larger events, togetherness and shared cultural experiences *and* series which sought to serve the needs of particular (niche) audience segments (see also Chap. 3).

CHALLENGE 3: GAINING VISIBILITY

A third challenge often highlighted by informants is that streaming makes it harder to *gain attention and visibility for drama series*, even the really good ones. NRK's Head of Television observed, 'One of the key challenges ahead, when we don't know how things are fragmented or how quickly people will change user habits, is to be able to make visible good projects we think the audience should discover' (Helsingen interviewed 2015). Relatedly, many mentioned the 'attention economy', in which attention is treated like currency (Goldhaber 1997) and media users 'spend' it according to their preferences for content that matched their interests and desires (Webster 2014). Many informants also reflected a notion of what Annette Hill terms 'roaming audiences', a metaphor used to capture how audiences traverse the media landscape following pathways created by the industry but also creating paths by themselves (2019: 11). Hence, the challenge is not only to make quality drama but also to make the audience aware of it and interested in it. NRK's Broadcasting Director lamented, 'Today, you can have world-class content, and there is still a chance that no one would discover it' (Eriksen interviewed 2019). This is partly a product of the publishing process in a streaming world: gaining visibility and exposure in an increasingly competitive market is hard, especially when one loses the ability to deploy scheduling strategies. Yet the informants insisted that NRK, as a public service broadcaster, has to succeed in attracting viewers: 'Our content has no value before it meets the audience' (Lund interviewed 2015).

NRK therefore had to experiment with new ways of attracting an audience and making it aware of NRK's content. One key strategy involved increased emphasis on shows which proved capable of *generating publicity and buzz*—that is, starting a public discourse around their content. One informant said, 'In a world of choice, content that distinguishes itself and creates buzz is good content' (Flesjø interviewed 2015). Press coverage, critics, reviews, nominations and prizes, as well as more general 'buzz' on social media (Facebook, Instagram, Twitter and Jodel), all played a huge part in turning the audience's attention towards forthcoming drama series, that is, they created pathways to that content (see also Chap. 4). Promotion and buzz have always been important to the television industry (Grainge and Johnson 2015), and this includes public service institutions. What the informants are describing as new is the *crucial* role of buzz and promotion, and a perception that buzz and promotion are increasingly crucial to the success (or failure) of a drama series. While the informants did not use the term 'paratext' themselves, they are describing a shift which is consistent with Jonathan Gray's use of the term to refer to surrounding texts—the 'greeters, gatekeepers, and cheerleaders for and of the media' who 'play the key role in determining if a text will sink or swim' (Gray 2010: 17, 39; see also Chap. 4). Consequently, many informants stressed that more time and energy is going towards tailoring promotion strategies to make sure good content becomes well known and for the right reasons—that is, to make sure that the audience knows what to expect and will encounter this content with the 'correct' (in NRK's view) expectations and 'reading strategies' (Gray 2010: 25). Likewise, informants noted the importance of public reviews, nominations and prizes, which would 'shadow' (Gray 2010: chapter 4) a drama series with positive expectations. Of course, such strategies are regularly applied by other players in the streaming television industry and perhaps most notably Netflix and HBO, who both work to increase nominations and prizes for their drama series to increase their critical acclaim. The shift here is in how critical such work was perceived to be for an incumbent public service institution such as NRK.

This focus on promotion has at least two key implications for the NRK. First, the need to share and promote content across various media platforms led to a situation where the lines between promotion and content become blurry, because good promotions have to be good content themselves in order to spread organically. Second, the use of social media to promote NRK content raises delicate discussions regarding how NRK shall relate to third-party platforms so as to make use of them without making them stronger competitors (see also Sundet et al. 2019).

Another frequently mentioned strategy to increase exposure and visibility was to build *audience engagement and fans.* This is not a new phenomenon within the television industry (Evans 2020; Harrington and Bielby 1995; Hill 2019; Hill and Steemers 2017; Jenkins 2006), and it has been a priority for Norwegian players for several decades (Maasø et al. 2007; see also Enli 2007; Kjus 2009). As Jonathan Gray and his colleagues write, 'rather than ridiculed, fan audiences are now wooed and championed by cultural industries' (2007: 4; see also Jenkins 2006; Pearson 2010). Loyal audiences and fans are thought to spread good content to others, meaning publicity and buzz will derive from a tighter industry–audience relation. Yet, audience engagement also goes deeper, as Annette Hill describes, 'engagement is more than capturing the attention of audiences, it is making a connection, and in some cases making a real difference to people's lives' (2019: 28; see also Evans 2020). Of course, NRK's goal is not always to 'make a real difference to people's lives', and various NRK divisions prioritised audience engagement to different degrees. Still, there is a general understanding among the informants that building a tighter, more deeply connected—and more *relevant*—relationship with the audience is important to NRK's success (see also Chap. 5).

CHALLENGE 4: SECURING CONTENT RIGHTS

Finally, many informants stressed that the 'world championship of television streaming' makes it harder to *attract and secure good content rights*. NRK's Head of Television said, 'Best content, best content rights—that's the most important for us in the future' (Helsingen interviewed 2015). While the quest for content rights is not new, streaming makes the issue both more dramatic and more complex. For one thing, many informants noted that television streaming requires content rights which are *long term and flexible* with regard to the platforms and publishing models they encompass. An audience which expected to watch what it wanted, *when* it wanted and *where* it wanted, they added, has obvious implications for what kind of content rights NRK needs in the first place. Furthermore, long-term, flexible content rights are important for strategic reasons, as they give NRK the leeway to experiment with new publishing models and ways of connecting with the audience. NRK's Head of Television explained, 'We don't want our content rights to decide our publishing choices. We don't know how the world will look in three years, and it would be stupid to invest a lot of money in something with limited rights' (Helsingen interviewed 2015). He then framed rights as decisive to the organisation's prospects: 'If I have content and rights, I can change our publishing strategy within a day' (Helsingen interviewed 2015). The informants also observed that younger audiences in particular expect content to be available on all platforms for a long time and have little tolerance for shorter 'windows' of availability such as those dictated by certain rights. Many informants thus insisted that they were no longer concerned with 'where our content is published first, but rather with how we manage to reach out to the widest audience possible' (Helsingen interviewed 2015), indicating a tendency towards neutrality in terms of publishing platforms, assuming that NRK owned and controlled them. To further highlight this point, NRK decided to only acquire television programmes which included the rights to publish both on linear channels and on demand. This strategy came with a cost, however, as NRK, during the ten-year analysis period, had to turn down a number of attractive international drama series because the online on-demand rights were already sold and only the linear rights were available.

Another complexity of the streaming world's rights situation for many informants was the fact that the competition for attractive content rights *intensified*, thanks to new globally oriented streaming services such as

Netflix and HBO. One informant said, 'The competition gets harder, and Netflix is clearly a part of it' (Flesjø interviewed 2015). The informants also pointed out that content rights and copyright had become areas of conflict in the globalised television-streaming world, particularly with regard to production and distribution. Many informants gave examples of drama series which were no longer available to buy for on-demand publishing because of Netflix and HBO. This is, of course, not a problem exclusive to NRK (for other examples, see Jenner 2018; Johnson 2019; Lobato 2019), but it was a new problem of sorts, given that NRK had long enjoyed a strong position from which to bargain for attractive international drama rights for the Norwegian television market.

For NRK, the increased competition for content rights led to at least two strategic shifts. First, there is an increased focus on programme exchanges and co-production arrangements as a means of securing content rights, ownership and control from the beginning (see also Hammett-Jamart et al. 2018). Hence, more emphasis is placed internally on producing and securing attractive drama series which can replace those now being acquired and controlled by international streaming services. Second, NRK prioritised the negotiation of long-term and flexible copyright agreements with national-interest organisations and institutions (such as the Norwegian Film Association, the Norwegian Writers' Guild and the Norwegian Actors' Association) to serve its own interest in the new streaming landscape. These negotiations are not without conflict, as many of these institutions claimed that NRK was paying too little and taking too much control in the streaming market. NRK maintained its strategy, however, arguing that securing content rights is crucial to its future success and essential to serving its audience effectively.

Summing Up

This chapter has analysed the ways in which key industry executives envision the impact of streaming on the making of television drama, pointing to four key challenges deriving from the fact that streaming breaks down territorial boundaries and changes the rules of the game from a 'national competition to a world championship'. They are as follows: first, the *challenge of retaining the audience* in an increasingly globalised television landscape where new (international) players are appearing and old scheduling principles are losing utility; second, the *challenge of creating 'world-class content'* to compete with bigger and more internationally oriented productions aimed at larger markets and boasting higher budgets; third, the *challenge of gaining visibility* amid a surplus of high-quality drama series, even when it is 'world-class content'; and fourth, *the challenge of securing long-term and flexible content rights* when the competition for television drama has become a 'global battlefield'. Streaming is clearly perceived to impact the production and publishing of television drama in fundamental ways, and the shifts are even more profound when they take place in the context of a small nation such as Norway (see also McElroy and Noonan 2019). Streaming, however, also presents opportunities in terms of new production models, publishing strategies and industry–audience relations, which will be further explored in the following three chapters.

These perceptions of change, taken for granted as they are, may well disguise yet other notions of streaming, both within NRK and elsewhere in the television industry. For example, NRK executives seemed to pigeonhole the drama audience as rational and goal-oriented in its search for high-quality content, perhaps at the expense of cultivating a more experimental audience approach or a more laissez-faire audience. Sometimes, for example, viewers just want something to run in the background while they are doing other things (Lull 1990; Morley 1992). It also became clear that NRK's commercial peers were unhappy with the emphasis NRK placed on retaining the audience—in terms of both viewing numbers and engagement and connectedness—and wanted NRK to take a less 'popular' route instead. There are different views on how broad or popular a public service broadcaster should be, and, in public debates, these views are often guided by strategic interests (Sundet and Syvertsen 2020). In the present study, however, the point is to uncover the conceptual frames and notions which guide drama-related strategies and actions, not to evaluate their accuracy or 'truthfulness'.

REFERENCES

Anderson, Benedict. 1991 [1983]. *Imagined Communities: Reflections on the Origin and Spread of Nationalism*. New York: Verso.

Ang, Ien. 2005 [1991]. *Desperately Seeking the Audience*. London and New York: Routledge.

Bjørn, Camilla. 2018. Head of NRK P3. In-Person Interview, Oslo, March 23.

blank. 2018–2019. NRK.

Bruun, Hanne. 2020. *Re-Scheduling Television in the Digital Era*. London and New York: Routledge.

Doyle, Gillian. 2016. Digitization and Changing Windowing Strategies in the Television Industry: Negotiating New Windows on the World. *Television & New Media* 17 (7): 629–645.

Elberse, Anita. 2013. *Blockbusters. Hit-Making, Risk-Taking, and the Big Business of Entertainment.* New York: Henry Holt Company.

Ellis, John. 2000. Scheduling: The Last Creative Act in Television? *Media, Culture & Society* 22 (1): 25–38.

Enli, Gunn. 2007. *The Participatory Turn in Broadcast Television. Institutional, Textual and Editorial Challenges and Strategies.* PhD thesis, University of Oslo.

Eriksen, Thor Gjermund. 2015. Hvordan skal NRK være relevant i fremtiden? *Aftenposten*, May 20.

———. 2019. Broadcasting Director at NRK. In-Person Interview, Oslo, March 14.

Ettema, James S., and D. Charles Whitney, eds. 1994. *Audiencemaking: How the Media Create the Audience.* London: Sage Publication.

Evans, Elizabeth. 2020. *Understanding Engagement in Transmedia Culture.* London and New York: Routledge.

Evens, Tom, and Karen Donders. 2018. *Platform Power and Policy in Transforming Television Markets.* Cham, Switzerland: Palgrave Macmillan.

Flesjø, Nicolay. 2015. Editorial Director of On-Demand Services at NRK. In-Person Interview, Oslo, January 26.

Frank, Robert H., and Philip J. Coock. 1995. *The Winner-Take-All Society. Why the Few at the Top Get so Much More Than the Rest of Us.* New York: Virgin Books.

Goldhaber, Michael H. 1997. Attention Shoppers! *Wired Magazine*, December 1.

Gray, Jonathan, Cornell Sandvoss, and C. Lee Harrington. 2007. Introduction: Why Study Fans?, In. *Fandom: Identities and Communities in a Mediated World*, eds. Jonathan Gray, Cornell Sandvoss, and C. Lee Harrington, 1–16. New York: New York University Press.

Grainge, Paul, and Catherine Johnson. 2015. *Promotional Screen Industries.* London and New York: Routledge.

Gray, Jonathan. 2010. *Show Sold Separately. Promos, Spoilers, and Other Media Paratexts.* New York: New York University Press.

Gulliksen, Hildri. 2017. Head of NRK Super. In-Person Interview, Oslo, May 19.

Hammett-Jamart, Julia, Petar Mitric, and Eva Novrup Redvall, eds. 2018. *European Film and Television Co-production: Policy and Practices.* London and New York: Palgrave Macmillan.

Harrington, C. Lee, and Denis D. Bielby. 1995. *Soap Fans. Pursuing Pleasure and Making Meaning in Everyday Life.* Philadelphia: Temple University Press.

Haugen, Vibeke Fürst. 2015. Head of Programming at NRK. In-Person Interview, Oslo, May 22.

Hauger, Knut Kristian. 2019. Dramaserien har fått et budsjett på rundt 150 millioner kroner. *Kampanje.com*, October 24.

Havens, Timothy, and Amanda D. Lotz. 2012. *Understanding Media Industries.* New York: Oxford University Press.

Hayes, Dade. 2020. Netflix Spending on Content Set to Climb Past $17B in 2020, Analyst Expects. *Deadline*, January 16.

Hedemann, Ole. 2014. *Ideutvikling i mediehuset*. Kristiansand: IJ-Forlaget.

———. 2018. *TV-formater. Fra Kvitt eller dobbelt til Skam*. Oslo: Cappelen Damm Akademiske.

Helsingen, Arne. 2015. Head of Television at NRK. In-Person Interview, Oslo, January 16.

Hill, Annette. 2019. *Media Experiences. Engaging with Drama and Reality Television*. London and New York: Routledge.

Hill, Annette, and Jeanette Steemers. 2017. Media Industries and Engagement. *Media Industries* 4 (1): 1–5.

Ihlebæk, Karoline A., Trine Syvertsen, and Espen Ytreberg. 2014. Keeping Them and Moving Them: TV Scheduling in the Phase of Channel and Platform Proliferation. *Television and New Media* 15 (5): 470–486.

Jayakar, Krishna, and David Waterman. 2000. The Economics of American Theatrical Movie Export: An Empirical Analysis. *Journal of Media Economics* 13 (3): 153–169.

Jenkins, Henry. 2006. *Convergence Culture. Where Old and New Media Collide*. New York and London: New York University Press.

Jenner, Mareike. 2018. *Netflix and the Re-invention of Television*. London: Palgrave Macmillan.

Johnson, Catherine. 2019. *Online TV*. London and New York: Routledge.

Kjus, Yngvar. 2009. *Event Media. Television Production Crossing Media Boundaries*. PhD thesis, University of Oslo.

Køhn, Ivar. 2017. Head of NRK Drama. In-Person Interview, Oslo, November 29.

Lilyhammer. 2012–2014. Rubicon TV for NRK and Netflix.

Lobato, Ramon. 2019. *Netflix Nations. The Geography of Digital Distribution*. New York: New York University Press.

Lotz, Amanda D. 2017. *Portals: A Treatise on Internet-Distributed Television*. Michigan Publishing.

Lull, James. 1990. *Inside Family Viewing: Ethnographic Research on Television's Audiences*. London: Routledge.

Lund, Øyvind. 2015. Head of Media at NRK. In-Person Interview, Oslo, February 4.

Lykkeland/State of Happiness. 2018–present. Maipo for NRK.

Maasø, Arnt, Trine Syvertsen, and Vilde Schanke Sundet. 2007. 'Fordi du fortjener det'. Publikumsdeltakelse som strategisk utviklingsområdet i mediebransjen. *Norsk medietidsskrift* 14 (2): 126–154.

McCabe, Janet, and Kim Akass, eds. 2007. *Quality TV. Contemporary American Television and Beyond*. New York: I.B. Tauris.

McElroy, Ruth, and Caitriona Noonan. 2019. *Producing British Television Drama. Local Production in a Global Era*. London: Palgrave Macmillan.

Michalsen, Gard L. 2017. Nok en gang lager NRK 'Norges dyreste dramaserie': 96 millioner kroner vil historien om oljeeventyret koste. *Medier24.no*, October 4.

Morley, David. 1992. *Television, Audiences and Cultural Studies*. London: Routledge.

Napoli, Philip M. 2011. *Audience Evolution: New Technologies and the Transformation of Media Audience*. New York: Columbia University Press.

NRK. 2014. *NRKs årsrapport 2014*. Oslo: NRK.

———. 2016. *NRKs langtidsstrategi 2016–2021*. Oslo: NRK.

Pearson, Roberta. 2010. Fandom in the Digital Era. *Popular Communication* 8 (1): 84–95.

Redvall, Eva Novrup. 2018. Reaching Young Audiences Through Research: Using the NABC Method to Create the Norwegian Web Teenage Drama *SKAM/ Shame*. In *True Event Adaptation*, ed. Davinia Thornley, 143–161. London and New York: Palgrave Macmillan.

Silverstone, Roger. 1999. *Why Study the Media?* London: Sage Publications.

SKAM/SHAME. 2015–2017. NRK.

Straubhaar, Joseph D. 2007. *World Television: From Global to Local*. Los Angeles: Sage Publication.

Sundet, Vilde Schanke, and Trine Syvertsen. 2020. From Problem to Solution? Why It Is Difficult to Restrict the Remit of Public Broadcasters. *International Journal of Cultural Policy*. Online First. https://doi.org/10.1080/1028663 2.2020.1807522.

Sundet, Vilde Schanke, and Espen Ytreberg. 2009. Working Notions of Active Audiences: Further Research on the Active Participant in Convergent Media Industries. *Convergence* 15 (4): 383–390.

Sundet, Vilde Schanke, Karoline Andrea Ihlebæk, and Kari Steen-Johnsen. 2019. Policy Windows and Converging Frames: A Longitudinal Study of Digitalization and Media Policy Change. *Media, Culture & Society* 42 (5): 711–726.

The Crown. 2016–present. Netflix.

Tolonen, Kristian. 2015. Head of Audience Insight at NRK. In-Person Interview, Oslo, February 6.

Van den Bulck, Hilde, and Hallvard Moe. 2017. Public Service Media, Universality and Personalization Through Algorithms: Mapping Strategies and Exploring Dilemmas. *Media, Culture & Society* 40 (6): 875–892.

Wallace, Petter. 2015. Head of External Productions at NRK. In-Person Interview, Oslo, January 15.

Webster, James G. 2014. *The Marketplace of Attention: How Audiences Take Shape in a Digital Age*. Cambridge, MA: MIT Press.

CHAPTER 3

Changing Production Cultures

Abstract This chapter discusses how streaming affects *television production*—that is, the ways in which television drama is produced to accommodate a more on-demand and potentially more international audience, including through new forms of partnerships, production models and storytelling techniques. It is organised according to three particular drama production models that streaming favours, which I have termed *going big, going small* and *going again*. Through analyses of these models, this chapter demonstrates that television streaming has increased the need for high-budget 'world-class' series but also smaller, more niche-oriented (online) drama productions, as well as drama remakes and adaptations. This chapter uses *Lilyhammer, SKAM* and *blank* to illustrate key tendencies and arguments.

Keywords *blank* • *Lilyhammer* • Production models • *SKAM* • Streaming • Television drama

INTRODUCTION

How does streaming affect the *production cultures* of television drama and what production models do streaming favour? Drawing upon the review of streaming-related industry perceptions in the previous chapter, this chapter will discuss three particular production models propelled by a changing television market, including their main opportunities and

V. S. Sundet, *Television Drama in the Age of Streaming*,
https://doi.org/10.1007/978-3-030-66418-3_3

51

challenges. The first model involves drama productions which are *going big*, aiming for larger, preferably transnational markets and audience groups via larger budgets and 'world-class' production values. *Lilyhammer* will serve as the example here; other, more well-known examples include *House of Cards* (Netflix, 2013–2018), *Game of Thrones* (HBO, 2011–2019) and *The Crown* (Netflix, 2019–present). The second model involves drama productions which are *going small*, aiming for more concentrated and niche-oriented (online) audience groups—often including youths—by strategically applying smaller budgets and selective but simpler production values. Both *SKAM* and *blank* serve as excellent examples here, though *SKAM* is better known. Obviously, 'going small' does not exclude 'going global', as *SKAM* and many other 'cult TV' productions have proven (see also Hills 2004). 'Going small' productions are nevertheless driven by a different production rationale and industry logic than 'going big' productions: both can go far, but for different reasons and via different routes and paths (see also Creeber 2011). The third model involves drama productions that are *going again*—that is, successors, adaptations and drama remakes (so-called scripted fiction) which build on existing success stories and try to replicate them. Both *blank* and the many *SKAM* remakes are good examples of this last model, seeking the success of the original using new storylines (*blank*) or the same storyline transposed into a new cultural context (the *SKAM* remakes). Other examples of 'going again' productions are *The Office* (BBC, 2001–2003) and *Broen/The Bridge* (SVT/DR, 2011–2018), as well as sequels and spinoffs which build on the universe or brand of previous successes—think of the web of films and television shows related to the Star Wars brand (Gray 2010; see also Chalaby 2016; Moran 2010; Oren and Shahaf 2012).

Streaming facilitates a wide range of drama productions, including productions not encompassed by the aforementioned three models. The main argument here is not that streaming shelves all other models but that it *favours* certain production logics—it fills them with opportunities. Another key argument is that streaming suits production models that point in different directions. The fact that these various production models can be found within the very same institution (NRK) strengthens the argument that they represent complementary, not competing, production strategies.[1]

---

[1] This chapter builds on in-depth case studies of the production models of *Lilyhammer*, *SKAM* and *blank*. The two first have been analysed in earlier publications, most importantly Sundet 2016 (*Still 'Desperately seeking the audience'? Audience making in the age of media*

GOING BIG: HIGH-BUDGET CO-PRODUCTIONS FOR THE WORLD

What I have termed 'going big' drama productions respond to the call for 'world-class content' described in Chap. 2: a perceived demand for higher quality, complexity and production value among 'unfaithful' audiences. 'Going big' productions also respond to the challenges involved in gaining visibility, as going big often means prioritising both promotion and branding to reach a larger (sometimes global) audience (see also Athique 2016; Doyle 2016; Hills et al. 2019). Some of these projects even become blockbusters—that is, large-budget productions aiming for a mass market and plenty of associated merchandising (Elberse 2013).

Lilyhammer is a good example of a 'going big' production. *Lilyhammer* was produced by Rubicon TV (owned by Endemol Shine Group) as an NRK/Netflix co-production. Netflix entered as a co-investor during the production of season 1 (in 2011), presumably to buttress the show's production budget and offer an international audience. The series received massive attention in the press in Norway, the United States and elsewhere, including coverage of Netflix's role and its novel production and distribution setup. The *New York Times*, for example, ran a story in 2012 claiming that *Lilyhammer* was launching 'streaming video's war on television' and noting that it represented a 'trailblazer and an interesting test case' for the binge-watching model (Hale 2012; see also Chap. 4). Similarly, *Rolling Stone* said the series 'marked the beginning of a brand new era of television' (Greene 2013).

According to informants, Netflix became a principal initiator of the increasing budget, which doubled with each new season, from season 1's 33 million NOK (€3.7 million) to season 2's 62 million NOK (€7 million) to season 3's 120 million NOK budget (€13.5 million) (Sundet 2017a). In addition to the international markets made available through Netflix, the distributor Red Arrow sold *Lilyhammer* internationally, and its first season would eventually appear in 130 countries (Hansen 2013). At the

convergence (the Lilyhammer *experience)*), Sundet 2017a (*Co-produced television drama and the cost of transnational 'success': The making of* Lilyhammer), Sundet 2019 (*From 'secret' online teen drama to international cult phenomenon: The global expansion of* SKAM *and its public service mission*) and Sundet 2020b (*'Will it translate?'—SKAM som remake* [*Will it translate?—SKAM as remake*]). The argument that streaming facilitates particular production models is also presented in Sundet 2020a (*Drama as flagship productions: Small-nation television and digital distribution*).

time, this made *Lilyhammer* NRK's most exported as well as most expensive drama series.

'Going big' productions have several opportunities and benefits for the partners involved, in which many of them are related to the fact that they are often international co-productions. Pil Gundelach Brandstrup and Eva Novrup Redvall (2005) distinguish among political benefits (such as creating a counterbalance against the US cultural hegemony), economic benefits (such as increasing the number of markets and private investors) and cultural-creative benefits (such as bringing people together through a shared sense of national culture and identity). In general, economic considerations outweigh the political and cultural ones (Selznick 2008: 17; see also Hammett-Jamart et al. 2018), especially for smaller nations such as Norway, which particularly appreciate the opportunity to share costs and increase market prospects. Furthermore, because international co-productions are intended to appeal to a 'multicultural' and 'transnational' audience, they are also expected to travel well to third markets, enhancing their market exposure even further (Selznick 2008: 19).

Lilyhammer brought several such opportunities to the partners involved (Sundet 2016). For NRK, it managed to garner a big national audience which also included young people—season 1 achieved a market share of over 55 per cent of the home market in Norway (Red Arrow 2012). Furthermore, its mix of genres (action, drama and comedy), unconventional style and play with both Norwegian and US stereotypes, especially in season 1, resonated well with NRK's values as a public service broadcaster. It also demonstrated NRK's ability to produce and commission 'world-class' content capable of attracting a transnational audience, which, at the time, was groundbreaking in and of itself. For Rubicon TV, *Lilyhammer* promptly became a high-profile signature programme with good ratings and reputation for which the production company could take credit. It also gave Rubicon TV first-hand experience with a high-budget television drama aimed at a transnational audience and produced in partnership with an increasingly important player—Netflix—in the globalised television market. Lastly, for Netflix, *Lilyhammer* represented attractive 'local' content at a time when the company was launching itself in the Nordic streaming market. Although Netflix is a key player in the global streaming market today, this was not the case when it joined the *Lilyhammer* team in 2011. One *Lilyhammer* Showrunner noted, 'I remember when *Lilyhammer* was sold to Netflix, and everyone said, "Netflix, what is that?"' (Bjørnstad interviewed 2015). Right away in 2012, however, just one year after joining the production of *Lilyhammer*, Netflix entered the Norwegian market with a flourish, using its investments to promote itself. *Lilyhammer* proved Netflix's ability to commission and co-produce 'original' popular content in partnership with local quality players, and it paved the way for later drama successes (see also Lobato 2019). A few years later, the CEO of Netflix reflected on the moment: 'We managed to make *Lilyhammer* popular across the globe, which taught us a lesson: "If we can do that with a Norwegian-English show with Steven Van Zandt in Lillehammer, what else can we achieve?"' (Hastings, quoted in Mohr 2018).

Co-productions can entail challenges and risks for stakeholders as well; previous studies have highlighted the loss of control (creative and economic) and of cultural specificity (and identity) as the most important of them (Hoskins and McFadyen 1993). While international co-productions are intended to speak to both a national and a transnational audience, they sometimes fail to do either (Renaud and Litman 1985). In a European context, this failure is often referred to as 'Europudding'—that is, something designed to please everyone that turns out to please no one. Other scholars frame international co-productions as cases of cultural imperialism or 'Americanisation'—one more way for Hollywood—or Netflix—to extend its power.

The co-production model of *Lilyhammer* trigged all the above-mentioned challenges, which manifested in three points of tension (Sundet 2017a). The first is an *economic* tension, concerning the production budget, which, as reported, doubled with each subsequent season. While Rubicon informants applauded the fact that an increasing budget allowed them to continue to make 'world-class' television, informants from NRK had mixed feelings about it, believing that *Lilyhammer* was intended to be a cost-effective and 'scruffy project' (Wallace interviewed 2015). Furthermore, the need for a growing budget shifted the power balance from NRK as the main investor in season 1 of *Lilyhammer* to Netflix as the main investor in season 3. A mutual interest in larger markets and budgets can motivate co-production arrangements, but it does not guarantee that stakeholders will agree upon either an ideal size for the budget or the best way to spend it, and *Lilyhammer* certainly gave NRK important insights into future co-production arrangements (Lund interviewed 2015; Wallace interviewed 2015).

The second tension is *legal*, and it manifested itself in discussions about content rights. It was put to test in season 3, when NRK decided to adopt Netflix's binge-publishing model of making all the episodes available online at once. Whereas NRK in *Lilyhammer*'s first two seasons followed a traditional broadcasting model—episodes were released weekly on both NRK's linear channel and its on-demand service—NRK changed its strategy in season 3: It still released weekly linear episodes, but it also made all the episodes available online at once. The move in season 3 was met with strong criticism from both Rubicon TV and Steven Van Zandt (who was often said to speak for Netflix), both of whom argued that NRK had gone beyond its legal rights (see also Eckblad and Hagen 2014). NRK, on the other hand, defended its right to binge-publish *Lilyhammer* in the context of its general obligation to publish content for the benefit of its audience (Flesjø interviewed 2015; Helsingen interviewed 2015). The fact that Netflix had gone from a small, mainly US-based streaming service to a truly international media player over the course of *Lilyhammer*'s three seasons and was now competing with NRK for both audiences and content rights may have informed NRK's decision as well. In the end, this legal tension around *Lilyhammer* taught an important lesson to NRK (and presumably Netflix) regarding the importance of negotiating flexible content rights in the globalised television market (see also Chap. 2).

The third tension is *culture-creative* and concerned with the show's identity. Though Netflix seldom gave notes on the script, and NRK did retain its primarily editorial responsibility through all three seasons, Netflix's participation did impact the production creatively. As one of the showrunners said, 'Netflix had a presence in that we knew *Lilyhammer* would air on Netflix' (Skodvin interviewed 2015). Of course, the increased production budget—which made Netflix the main investor in seasons 2 and 3—may also have made a difference. Many informants, for example, referred to debates regarding the appropriate amount of explicit and unjustified violence, sex and bad language in *Lilyhammer* (Rønning interviewed 2015; Wallace interviewed 2015). In a US context, these things tended to be equated with quality, because they signalled greater ambition and more creativity than what was associated with more risk-averse networks (DeFino 2014). In a Western European public service context, though, this was not the case (Rønning interviewed 2015). In all, these conversations centred around what kind of show *Lilyhammer* was meant to be and for whom: Was it a television 'dramedy' aimed at a Norwegian public service audience or an American action drama aimed at a Netflix pay-TV audience (see also Sundet 2016)? That said, the stakeholders continued to agree that the show should remain culturally anchored in local (Norwegian) culture as a key selling point. Van Zandt insisted:

I wanted it (*Lilyhammer*) to be as Norwegian as possible. (…) If you focus on nuance and detail and the things that have a local interest, those are the most universal. Those are the things that people gravitate towards and love to see. (Steven Van Zandt, actor and executive producer of *Lilyhammer*, quoted in Radish 2013)

Hence, while a key selling point of *Lilyhammer* within the Norwegian context was its cultural proximity, precisely the show's 'Norwegianness' was seen as a key selling point abroad. This finding resonates well with other studies of Nordic drama exports, which finds that the experience of *differences*—'the aesthetic of the exotic' (Jacobsen and Jensen 2020: 11)—is just as crucial as the experience of cultural *closeness* in explaining international success (see also Hill 2019; Weissmann 2012).

To summarise, *Lilyhammer* represents a 'going big' production in terms of how NRK used it to team up with the 'big guys' to go for bigger (international) audiences through higher production values and 'world-class content'. It proved for both NRK and Rubicon TV that international markets and 'world-class budgets' were within reach, and it paved the way for a new set of Nordic Netflix/HBO co-productions (see also NFI 2018). For example, five years after *Lilyhammer* ended, the same showrunners (Anne Bjørnstad and Eilif Skodvin) and production company (Rubicon TV) premiered HBO Nordic's first original series, *Beforeigners* (HBO, 2019–present). In this show, the storyline centres around time travellers from the past who appear in the capital of Norway. Like *Lilyhammer*, this series was locally rooted but confronted universal dilemmas—it was a 'going big' production.

Going Small: Online Drama Based on Audience Needs

What I have termed 'going small' productions aim for more niche-oriented (online) audience groups and typically feature smaller budgets and simpler production values. They respond well to the call for relevance and audience insight described in Chap. 2, where many informants highlighted the fact that a unique knowledge of Norwegian audiences and culture had become NRK's key selling point. Both *SKAM* and *blank* are perfect examples of going small productions; both applied small budgets to content which targeted a narrow audience segment—Norwegian sixteen-year-old girls (*SKAM*) and Norwegian nineteen-year-old youths (*blank*).

Furthermore, they both draw upon extensive audience research to identify needs and inform relevant and realistic portrayals of their characters (Faldalen 2016; see also Sundet 2019).

Production-wise, both *SKAM* and *blank* built on an online drama format originally developed in NRK's children division (NRK Super) starting in 2007 to tell daily fictional stories to young girls—*Sara* (2008–2009), *MIA* (2010–2012) and *Jenter/Girls* (2013–2018). The goal was to 'bring back' a target group that otherwise was distancing itself from NRK (Gulliksen interviewed 2017; Wisløff interviewed 2018). The format reflected the contemporary focus on blogs and YouTube as tools for self-branding (Magnus 2016: 32) and took its lead from digital and transmedia storytelling as well (Jenkins 2006; Evans 2011; see also Chap. 4). These early projects exhibited characteristics which would later become the key features of both *SKAM* and *blank*: they were character-driven online drama series in which the storyline was told in daily instalments and in real-time on a blog through a mix of video clips, messages and pictures. The audience, in turn, was invited to comment and engage (see Fig. 3.1, see also Sundet 2019). All these series also celebrated innovation and had an outspoken goal of trying new things. As explained by one founder of the format, 'online drama has always been different and experimental. (…) "Can we test this? I hear someone did this, let's try"' (Wisløff interviewed 2018). Of course, smaller audience groups and budgets, combined with low expectations, probably helped to foster an experimental mindset. As the same informant said, 'nobody paid us close attention or thought we could become a great success, so we could do almost anything we wanted' (Wisløff interviewed 2018). The fact that this format was developed within a division already known for its innovative approach to both new-media platforms and storytelling may have had an impact as well (Gulliksen interviewed 2017; see also Andersen and Sundet 2019).

Figure 3.1 illustrates *SKAM* as an online drama told through a mix of video clips, chat messages and Instagram pictures on the *SKAM* website (skam.p3.no)

The three first series (*Sara*, *MIA* and *Jenter*) all proved incredibly popular within their target audience (girls aged ten to thirteen years) but gained little attention with other audience segments or the media, earning *MIA* the label 'one of NRK's most secret successes' (Nyborg 2012). *SKAM*, on the other hand, transformed throughout its four seasons from a 'secret' online teen drama—carefully avoiding official promotions in favour of the power of word-of-mouth—to a global cult phenomenon

Fig. 3.1 *SKAM* as online drama

with viewers and fans of all ages around the world (Sundet 2019; see also Krüger and Rustad 2019; Lindtner and Dahl 2019). *SKAM* also became a beloved topic on various social media sites (Facebook, Twitter, Instagram, YouTube, Tumblr, Jodel, etc.), where fan activities ranged from serious discussions of key themes to interpretations of intertextual references, speculations about future narratives, selfies with and gossip about the actors, and fan-produced fiction, art, memes and gifs (see Chap. 5; see also Petersen and Sundet 2019; Sundet and Petersen 2020). In fact, *SKAM* illustrates well Annette Hill's term 'roaming audiences', that is, audiences as 'pathmakers, roaming around storytelling as viewers, users and producers' in which their movements 'suggest a right to roam' (2019: 31).

The novelty of *SKAM* attracted a lot of attention within the television industry and in the press, including the *Guardian* story 'Shame: A Scandi TV Sensation for the Social Media Generation' (Hughes 2016) and the *Vanity Fair* story 'Is This Norwegian TV Series the Future of Television?' (Bradley 2016; see also McDermott 2017). Several media outlets called *SKAM* the most important show of the year, thanks to the ways it dealt with difficult (teen) issues and presented in a novel form (see, e.g. Aldrige 2016; Atkinson 2016; Bakare 2016; Hegnsvad 2016; Perkins 2017). Following the explosion of interest from fans, the mainstream media and the trade press, international broadcasters and publishers began to pay attention as well, and during 2017 *SKAM* was ultimately sold for remakes in six European countries as well as the United States, where it was distributed in the spring of 2018 as the 'first Facebook Watch' TV show (Donadio 2016; see also Max 2018). NRK learned from the show's success as well and initiated several new online dramas following in its footsteps, including *blank*, *Lovleg* (Rubicon TV/NRK, 2018–2019) and *LikMeg/ LikMe* (NRK, 2018–present). As explained by the Head of NRK P3, 'I think *SKAM* is the ultimate proof that we need to make our content "choosable" and listen to the audience, instead of just broadcasting content' (Bjørn interviewed 2018; see also Andersen and Sundet 2019).

In the same way that 'going big' productions bring with them certain opportunities and challenges, 'going small' productions do the same, and in the latter, the opportunities and challenges were often strongly interlinked. The first opportunity (that was also a challenge) was related to these shows' heavy use of *audience insight*. As mentioned, all of NRK's online formats relied upon extensive audience feedback which, in the case of *SKAM*, included 50 in-depth interviews with Norwegian teens from all over the country, 200 speed interviews, school visits, social media scanning, and readings of reports and statistics regarding teen culture (Sundet 2019). The aim was to gain insight into Norwegian teens in order to portray them in a relevant and authentic way but also to discover ways in which these new online drama concepts could serve the needs of their particular audience segments (Magnus interviewed 2017; Næsheim interviewed 2017; Wisløff interviewed 2018). For example, the online drama series strove to tackle serious issues which arose through audience research and supply viable ways to cope with and 'work through' (Ellis 2000: 124) everyday challenges and dilemmas (Andresen 2014). As *blank*'s Assistant Scriptwriter put it:

> In our interviews, the target group members state very clearly that they feel alone, many for the first time, and I can remember that feeling. I hope these 'kids' will dare to hold all feelings without it being so scary. Today, it is such a defeat to feel bad, because everything is set up for perfection. (…) I hope they will feel normally lonely and understand that *that* feeling will not last forever. (Hege Nordlie, *blank*'s Assistant Scriptwriter, interviewed 2017)

These productions even formulated 'mission statements' which defined their visions in response to their audiences' needs. For instance, *SKAM*'s mission statement read, '*SKAM* aims to help 16-year-old girls, strengthen their self-esteem through dismantling taboos, making them aware of interpersonal mechanisms, and showing them the benefits of confronting their fears' (Furevold-Boland interviewed 2016). Similarly, *blank*'s mission statement read as follows:

Our aim is to give nineteen-year-olds strong and identifiable characters who overcome external and internal barriers to their own development and who dare to face rejection and rise after defeat. In doing so, we will help them take ownership of their own lives in a new and insecure period and show them how to welcome love. (Internal working document, 17.08.2017, my translation)

Backing these formats' extensive use of audience insight was an abiding faith in cultural proximity but also a notion that the younger audience would prioritise relevance over 'conventional quality'. The Head of NRK Super explained, 'It's not that important to them [children] that we spend big money on lighting. What matters to them is that our content feels *relevant*' (Gulliksen interviewed 2017). Similarly, one of the founders of the online drama explained, 'A key reasons why online drama succeeds, is because it is about real Norwegian girls and their everyday life. (…) I think Norwegian girls feel these girls are more representative to them than the "Netflix-girls"' (Wisløff interviewed 2018). This sentiment was also echoed by *SKAM*'s Online Producer:

We were aiming for an audience that does not feel at home at NRK and in competition with the world. Our strength is that we know the society they grow up in. We have the opportunity to dive deep, get to know them and understand them. (Mari Magnus, *SKAM*'s Online Producer, interviewed 2017)

An overriding emphasis on audience insight and realism and relevance brought challenges as well. For example, many *blank* informants stressed the complexities of going close and remaining relevant when the target audience lived different lives. *blank*'s Showrunner—who also wrote and directed season 1—said:

In the previous online dramas—*Sara*, *MIA*, *Jenter* and *SKAM*—the target group lived more or less similar lives, at least on the outside, and they shared reality with the main character; they go to school, they meet friends. (…) When you reach nineteen, the target group becomes far more diverse—they live different lives. (…) Whatever we do, we will not be able to be representative for very many. (Knut Næsheim, *blank*'s Showrunner, interviewed 2017)

Of course, the goal of realism could also conflict with the storyline's need for action and drama; in the case of *blank*, for example, the production team faced criticism for a story which was too realistic and consequently, according to some members of the audience, too boring. One audience member was perhaps too candid in the comments section following season 1 blog updates, while clearly comparing *blank* with *SKAM*: 'Incredibly dull. Nothing happens. I am missing music, missing action, missing excitement. Pathetic, boring, not interesting, the lover is anti-caring. This is nothing' (my translation).

A second opportunity with online drama—which also represented challenge—was the way the format's real-time publishing model introduced a *sense of 'liveness'*, which differentiated these shows from both standard weekly TV release schedules and Netflix's binge-publishing model. As will be further elaborated in the next chapter, real-time publishing means that the time and date in the series followed the time and date for the audience, making the production's rhythm irregular, unpredictable and addictive. It forces audiences to keep an eye out for updates while generating a sense of authenticity and liveness as they share in the lives of the characters. Furthermore, this publishing model, combined with the show's main character's point of view, strengthens the audience's identification with the central protagonist and the story world (see also Jerslev 2017; Sundet 2017b). One NRK informant noted, 'The main point of real-time drama is to get into the viewer's life in such a way that they during the day will stop and think "has there been a new clip yet?" and "I wonder how they are doing?"' (Fossbakken interviewed 2017).

Real-time drama publishing also had challenges. Several informants found it a difficult format to master because the storyline had to deal with the aspect of time as though it were real. The Assistant Scriptwriter for *blank* said, 'I have never thought so much about form as now—how much form guides content. (…) I find so much content *not* fitting into the real-time formula' (Nordlie interviewed 2017). Likewise, *blank's* Project Leader asked:

> Taking a parallel to the golden age of Hollywood: How long did it take to learn to write a Western? How many Western movies did you have to see before you could make one yourself? And that's only a manuscript without the platform or the digital reality. (Åse Marie Hole, Project Leader of *blank*, interviewed 2017)

Furthermore, many informants stressed that the real-time format—where the content was written and produced only weeks before it was published by a small production team on a low budget—hardly was a sustainable production model (Bettvik interviewed 2017; Hole interviewed 2017; Wisløff interviewed 2018). On average, *SKAM* filmed two manuscripts (one manuscript per episode) in only three days, while *blank* filmed two manuscripts in four days (Bettvik interviewed 2017). Furthermore, many of these productions operate under the premise that the most coherent real-time universes were created if the same 'auteur' both wrote and directed these shows (Faldalen 2016). This, of course, made the workload almost unbearable for the showrunners. As one informant with experience form both *SKAM* and *bank* explained, 'it is complicated when Knut [showrunner of *blank*] has to be three places in the storyline at once—he is out shooting and directing, at the same time as he is in the editing room editing what he has just done *and* writing what is to come' (Bettvik interviewed 2017). Over time, NRK tested various models to organise and produce these shows more sustainable, including models that spill the role of writer and director (Wisløff interviewed 2018; Hole interviewed 2018). However, both *SKAM* and *blank* (season 1) followed 'the auteur model' with Julie Andem and Knut Næsheim as the two shows' showrunners. As one informant concluded, 'the online drama formula is a success formula, but it is also the opposite because it is not a sustainable way to work. It requires us to be few, but the fact that we are few makes it too much work for each person' (Fossbakken interviewed 2017).

A third opportunity (which also represented a challenge) was the *dialogue with the audience* (see also Chap. 5). As one informant explained, 'the dialogue with the audience in the comments section is like drugs. [laughter] You realise that what you are making means things to people' (Molstad interviewed 2017). Several informants appreciated the way in which this particular mode of storytelling fed on the audience's response and noted that the production team would enter into a cat-and-mouse game with the audience in which they left Easter eggs, clues and codes for the audience to solve and play with (Akrim interviewed 2018; Erlandsen interviewed 2017; Øverlie interviewed 2017). Because these shows were written and produced only weeks before they were published, the team was also able to adjust storylines based on audience feedback. For instance, one informant explained how *SKAM* actively used audience feedback to keep the storyline unpredictable: 'When everyone in the audience think something is going to happen, you do the opposite instead. If we had published everything in advance, we would lose the flexibility that audience feedback gives' (Bettvik interviewed 2017). In both *SKAM* and *blank*, there was an unwritten agreement between these shows and their audiences that the production team would at the very least read all the comments on the shows' websites (skam.p3.no, blank.p3.no) on a daily basis. While the audience did not always get what it asked for, the production team became better storytellers by knowing what the audience thought it wanted (Magnus interviewed 2017; see also Lentz 2017; Nyborg 2012). One informant said, 'If you are good enough, you have a continuous focus group talking to you, commenting on what you make and sharing it' (Aspeflaten interviewed 2017). This cultivated synergy with the audience was also seen as an efficient way to promote these types of series, as fans would spread the word among themselves (Øverlie interviewed 2017; Sprus interviewed 2018).

Figure 3.2 illustrates how the *SKAM* team entered a dialogue with audiences and fans, among others by incorporating comments and feedback from the fandom. Here exemplified by a scene from season 4, where the production team re-created a fan drawing originally posted on a fan's Instagram account (@elli_skam) only months before. Fan drawing used with permission.

Entering into such a dialogue with the audience also had its downside, both for the production teams and for the actors. Keeping up with the audience was time consuming and could neglect other pressing issues. In addition, not everyone was fond of getting direct feedback every day, and some found their professional instincts contested or disturbed: 'I find it hard to balance how much we should change based on audience response and how much we should stick to what had been planned' (Nordlie interviewed 2018). Reading audience responses was not always a pleasant experience, as the fan community could be critical and even hateful (see also

Fig. 3.2   *SKAM* as entering a dialogue with audiences and the fans

Gray 2003). The Assistant Scriptwriter at *blank* explained, 'I had to take a break from the comment section after my first week moderating because my heart hurt reading it. It was not only because people were angry at us or the show, but also towards each other' (Nordlie interviewed 2018). For the young actors, the audience feedback could be particularly hard to handle. As explained by one of the actors, whose character received a lot of criticism in the comments section:

> In the beginning, it got to me; I was not prepared. I know he is a character I play, but since we are so alike, it was still a bit close to home. When you have a character in a theatre or a film, you have a larger process building it further away from you. Here it was a bit, like, 'oh'. (William Arnø, actor in *blank*, interviewed 2018)

Even actors playing more popular characters found audience response on social media challenging: 'Simen [the character he played] has almost only received positive comments, but when you read them, it is easy to think that people are a bit crazy' (Fort interviewed 2018). Similarly, another actor described how some members of the audience would transfer the intimacy they felt to the characters to the actors: 'Suddenly you have to deal with people thinking they know you. Everything online I can handle, but it feels strange when people start approaching me and hugging me in real-life' (Maurud interviewed 2018). Even worse than criticism, however, was silence, said one informant with experience with both *SKAM* and *blank*: 'Getting criticism in the comment section is not the worst. The worst is when nothing happens there. (…) It is the silence that is cruel' (Molstad interviewed 2017).

To summarise, *SKAM*, *blank* and the other real-time online drama series capture the ethos of 'going small' productions in terms of their low budgets and orientation towards a niche audience. While the ongoing expansion of a global streaming market has boosted production budgets as well, these innovative, cost-efficient, niche drama series represent a thriving trend. They do not achieve their competitive edge by applying traditional production values but by being relevant and innovative to the intended audience—a new way of thinking about niche (teen) drama in the blockbuster era. Furthermore, their small, distinct audience groups give them the opportunity to go close. As shown, the gains are potentially tremendous, but they are not without costs.

GOING AGAIN: SCRIPTED FICTION AND DRAMA REMAKES

What I have termed 'going again' productions involve sequels, adaptations and drama remakes (so-called scripted fiction) that build on recent success stories and try to replicate them. Both *blank* and the many *SKAM* remakes are good examples of this category, as they aimed to repeat the success of the original format but with new storylines (*blank*) or with the same storyline translated into new cultural contexts (the *SKAM* remakes). As of 2019, seven *SKAM* remakes have been released, making *SKAM* one of the most exported drama formats in the world and certainly NRK's most exported drama format (Hedemann 2018). Six of the remakes were made for European producers—*SKAM France, Druck, SKAM Italia, SKAM NL, SKAM Espania* and *WtFock* (Carlström 2017)—whereas *SKAM Austin* was made in a US context but distributed to a global audience via Facebook Watch (Max 2018).[2] All these remakes premiered in 2018 or one year after the original *SKAM* concluded.

The emphasis on scripted fiction, adaptations and drama remakes can be linked to the establishment of the 'format industry' in the 2000s (Chalaby 2016). The literature on television formats—typically focused on reality and entertainment shows—shows that formats give several opportunities for producers involved that are generally linked to economic, promotional and risk-reducing aspects (Waisbord 2007). To start with, television formats offer the prospect of repeating another country's success story while enjoying closer cultural proximity and enhanced 'authenticity'. Several studies have shown that audiences prefer to watch national programmes in their own language but care less about where the original idea was developed (Straubhaar 2007). Other studies have demonstrated that television formats are usually more affordable than original productions, because producers can buy them ready-made and thus save time on development and pre-production work (Waisbord 2007: 380).

---

[2] Why did NRK sell *SKAM* as a format and not as an original drama series to be subtitled or dubbed for its international markets? One important reason was *SKAM*'s extensive use of music—more than 200 songs were used across its four seasons, many from popular and international artists. This made it 'close to impossible' (Lang-Ree interviewed 2017) for NRK to acquire the music rights necessary to resell *SKAM* as an original production, and even if NRK had managed to acquire the rights, they would have been too expensive. As the music played an important role in *SKAM*—many of the scenes were written for particular songs—cutting or changing the music was out of the question (Lang-Ree interviewed 2017; Fossbakken interviewed 2017; see also Sundet 2020b).

Moreover, formats represent reduced risk, because they have been tested in their original markets (Waisbord 2007: 380), and they are already known brands, which helps their promotion (Hedemann 2018: 21; see also Grainge and Johnson 2015).

Scripted fictions—or drama remakes—are less common than reality and entertainment formats for several reasons. They typically have higher budgets and associated risks, making their economic benefits less assured (Hedemann 2018: 120; see also Chalaby 2016). Besides, they are often more complex and culture specific, meaning they can be harder to 'translate' into new cultural contexts (Waisbord 2007: 288). Their sales situation is also complex, in that sales of drama remakes can hinder export sales of the original show, which are needed to offset these series' high budgets (Hedemann 2018: 120). Lastly, drama remakes seem less ambitious than original (national) stories, and this is an issue for institutions with a public service mandate (Hedemann 2018: 43).

Nevertheless, drama remakes offer several opportunities to producers— most importantly, they allow for the retelling of a popular and attractive story to local audiences, in the local language, with enhanced cultural proximity. The *SKAM* format also had some distinct features which made it especially attractive (Sundet 2020b). To start with, it had proven extremely successful at *attracting younger audiences*, which became a key selling point (Hedemann interviewed 2017).[3] The fact that *SKAM* also managed to become a strong brand among youth globally explains why many of its remakes kept the *SKAM* name instead of translating it to the respective local language. Second, *SKAM* had a strong 'track record' in its home market—in terms of market shares, ratings and general buzz— which *promised a larger audience* beyond the teens it targeted. This was true not only in Norway but also in the other Scandinavian countries, where *SKAM* broke streaming records (Birk 2017; Nylander 2017; Woldsdal and Michelsen 2016). As such, the *SKAM* format was seen as a successful deliverer of viewers from linear channels to digital, on-demand platforms—a high priority for producers, broadcasters and distributors alike in a competitive streaming landscape. Third, *SKAM* represented a *new way of producing real-time online drama*, which was considered 'the sensation for the social media generation' (Hughes 2016) and 'the future

---

[3] For instance, when NRK surveyed Norwegian teens after season 2, 98 per cent of people between fifteen and twenty-nine years of age reported knowing about the show, and close to 70 per cent reported having seen it (Sørensen 2017: 18–19).

of television' (Bradley 2016; see also McDermott 2017). Hence, the *SKAM* format promised to be attractive teen drama with general high ratings *and* an opportunity to learn new ways of storytelling. Simon Fuller at XIX Entertainment stressed the second point as an important reason for his interest in the *SKAM* format rights for the US market: 'This show packs a punch and is leading the way in exploring multi-platform storytelling' (quoted in Bronson 2016). Facebook's head of creative strategy added, 'When I first heard about *SKAM*, it felt like I was seeing the future of storytelling' (Van Veen, quoted in Clarke 2017). The fact that *SKAM* was produced on a low budget with a small production team helped make it a less risky wager as well.

The *SKAM* remakes (and *blank* project) also had some challenges above and beyond the general difficulties with scripted formats described above (Sundet 2020b). To start with, producers struggled with the online real-time format based on audience feedback, precisely because it represented a *new way of storytelling*. While Julie Andem and the original *SKAM* team spent several years perfecting it, the *SKAM* remake teams had less experience to rely on. Similar issues were noted by many *blank* informants, even those who had previously worked with online drama:

> I think it's impossible to learn how to make online drama without actually doing it for a season. We used three quarters of a year preparing social media content for season 1, but in the end, we had to throw most of it away and make it as we went along. We needed to see the videos and the audience response together to make good content. (Henrik Aspeflaten, *blank*'s Online Producer, interviewed 2018)

Another challenge arose from the format's goal of using extensive audience research to place the *storyline close to reality* and privilege relevance and authenticity (Magnus 2016). As already described, all these online drama series built on extensive audience research about Norwegian teens to create both key characters and storylines. For the *SKAM* remakes, relevance and authenticity meant balancing *SKAM*'s original vision and core stories—developed based on Norwegian teens and their interests and needs—against the unique conditions and demands of the local teen culture to which the series was being transposed. Production teams had to know their local youth culture *and* be able to translate the *SKAM* premise to fit into it.

A third challenge with the *SKAM* remakes was ironically tied to the show's strong *brand and fan base*. As already described, the international fan base was important in exporting *SKAM* outside of Norway. However, the global fandom sometimes stood in the way of new viewers of *SKAM* remakes by, for example, spoiling the narrative twists and turns. The thrill, excitement and surprises many viewers experienced while watching *SKAM* the first time were harder to pull off in the *SKAM* remakes. For some new fans, the *SKAM* remakes also came across as unnecessary complex as they tried to service 'old' fans who were already familiar with the *SKAM* universe. The series overtly positioned its fans as social media 'hunters and gatherers' (Jenkins 2006: 21), but this attitude risked going over the heads of the newcomers. This was also an issue for the *blank* team, which struggled to stay focused on and relevant to the target audience of Norwegian nineteen-year-olds without getting co-opted by the most active Scandinavian *SKAM* fans, many of whom were in their thirties and forties (see also Petersen and Sundet 2019). As one audience member wrote in *blank*'s comment section, 'hoping this does not become as popular as *SKAM*. If so, there will only be people around thirty-plus screaming out analysis and theories and destroying the comment section' (my translation). Another joined in, 'Hello creators. For your own sake, try to avoid parents from getting hold of this show. It was not the same when my mother started posting how much she liked Noora (like everyone else)' (my translation). In short, both *blank* and the *SKAM* remakes had to balance the need to serve a local teen audience with the demands and expectations of more experienced—and, sometimes, older—fans (see also Chap. 5; Sundet and Petersen 2020).

Both *blank* and the *SKAM* remakes thus represent 'going again' productions with their associated economic, promotional and risk-reducing opportunities. As the preceding analysis has shown, these productions shed new light on the practices required for a globalised streaming market. While scripted formats and drama remakes are not new, Scandinavian productions such as *SKAM* are leading the way in both innovations and audience penetration (Hedemann 2018: 121–125), though many challenges remain.

SUMMING UP

This chapter has analysed some of the ways in which streaming affects production models of television drama. I have described them as going big, going small and going again. A key argument is that television streaming facilitates both big-budget drama series which target larger, transnational audiences and small-budget drama series which target more niche-oriented audiences. This chapter shed light on how these productions all expand towards international markets but in different ways and through different routes (from Steven Van Zandt, Netflix and Red Arrow for *Lilyhammer* to international fans and trade press for *SKAM* and the *SKAM* remakes) and how they renegotiate their local and cultural distinctiveness when crossing national borders. Furthermore, this chapter pointed to how local authenticity work as a key selling point in both national and international markets, in which it in the latter becomes the 'aesthetic of the exotic' (Jacobsen and Jensen 2020: 11). This chapter also highlighted how these productions all aim to serve a Norwegian audience but increasingly enter into partnerships with private and commercial players to do so—for example, the co-production partnerships of *Lilyhammer* or the use of social media platforms (Instagram and YouTube) of *SKAM* and *blank*. Partnerships as such were not without tensions, but were nevertheless understood to be important for increasing budget and markets (*Lilyhammer*) and serving the audience where they were (*SKAM* and *blank*). As will be further discussed in the next chapter, these production models also represent different distribution strategies, including the binge-publishing model of *Lilyhammer* and the real-time publishing model of *SKAM* and *blank*.

REFERENCES

Akrim, Rashid. 2018. Online Designer on *SKAM* and *blank* at NRK P3 Event and Development, in-person interview, Oslo, 6 March.
Aldrige, Øystein. 2016. NRK treffer blink fra skolegården. *Aftenposten*, 12 January.
Andersen, Mads Møller Tommerup, and Vilde Schanke Sundet. 2019. Producing Online Youth Fiction in a Nordic Public Service Context. *VIEW Journal of European Television History and Culture* 8 (6): 110–125.
Andresen, Øystein Espeseth. 2014. Hva er NRKs 'Jenter'? *NRK.no*, 20 June.
Arnø, William Greni. 2018. Actor on *blank* at NRK, in-person interview, Oslo, 28 June.

Aspeflaten, Henrik. 2017. Online Producer on *blank* and Assistant Online Producer on *SKAM* at NRK, in-person interview, Oslo, 27 September.

———. 2018. Online Producer on *blank* and Assistant Online Producer on *SKAM* at NRK, in-person interview, Oslo, 26 June.

Athique, Adrian. 2016. *Transnational Audiences. Media Reception on a Global Scale*. Cambridge: Polity.

Atkinson, Sophie. 2016. Why Norway's Most Hyped Show 'Skam' Isn't 'Skins' But You Should Watch it Anyway. *Highsnobiety*, 22 December.

Bakare, Lanre. 2016. Skam: The Norwegian Hit that Could Take US TV into Uncharted Territory. *The Guardian*, 13 December.

Beforeigners. 2019–present. Rubicon TV for HBO Nordic.

Bettvik, Ida. 2017. Production Leader on *SKAM* (S4) and *blank* at NRK, in-person interview, Oslo, 24 November.

Birk, Trine. 2017. Vi er vilde med *SKAM*: Norsk seerhit slår ny record. *DR.no*, 27 January.

Bjørn, Camilla. 2018. Head of NRK P3, in-person interview, Oslo, 23 March.

Bjørnstad, Anne. 2015. Showrunner on *Lilyhammer* at Rubicon TV, in-person interview, Oslo, 18 February.

blank. NRK. 2018–2019.

Bradley, Laura. 2016. Is This Norwegian TV Series the Future of Television? *Vanity Fair*, 9 December.

Brandstrup, Pil Gundelach, and Eva Novrup Redvall. 2005. Breaking the Borders: Danish Coproductions in the 1990s. In *Transnational Cinema in a Global North: Nordic Cinema in Transition*, eds. Andrew Nestingen and Trevor G. Elkington, 141–164. Detroit: Wayne State University Press.

Broen/Bron/The Bridge. SVT/DR. 2011–2018.

Bronson, Fred. 2016. Simon Fuller to Produce English Version of Norwegian Teen Drama 'Shame'. *Hollywood Reporter*, 8 December.

Carlström, Wilhelm. 2017. Six Countries Set for Remakes of Norway's Hit Show Skam—And the American Version will Air on Facebook's Watch Service. *Nordic Business Insider*, 18 October.

Chalaby, Jean K. 2016. Drama without Drama: The Late Rise of Scripted TV Formats. *Television & New Media* 17 (1): 3–20.

Clarke, Stewart. 2017. Facebook Orders Online Teen Drama 'Skam'. Simon Fuller behind the English-language Remake of Innovative, Online Drama. *Variety*, 18 October.

Creeber, Glen. 2011. It's Not TV, It's Online Drama: The Return of the Intimate Screen. *International Journal of Cultural Studies* 14 (6): 591–606.

DeFino, Dean J. 2014. *The HBO Effect*. New York: Bloomsbury.

Donadio, Rachel. 2016. Will 'Skam', a Norwegian Hit, Translate? *New York Times*, 9 December.

Doyle, Gillian. 2016. Digitization and Changing Windowing Strategies in the Television Industry: Negotiating New Windows on the World. *Television & New Media* 17 (7): 629–645.

Druck. Bantry Bay Production for ZDF. 2018–present.

Eckblad, Bjørn, and Anders W. Hagen. 2014. NRK hisset på seg Netflix. *Dagens Næringsliv*, 15 December.

Elberse, Anita. 2013. *Blockbusters. Hit-making, Risk-taking, and the Big Business of Entertainment*. New York: Henry Holt Company.

Ellis, John. 2000. *Seeing Things. Television in the Age of Uncertainty*. London: I.B.Tauris.

Erlandsen, Kim. 2017. Online Developer on *SKAM* and *blank* at NRK P3 Event and Development, in-person interview, Oslo, 30 November.

Evans, Elizabeth. 2011. *Transmedia Television*. New York: Routledge.

Faldalen, Jon Inge. 2016. -Nerven i 'Skam' skal være sterk og relevant. *Rushprint. no*, 4 April.

Fort, Jakob Larsen. 2018. Actor on *blank* at NRK, in-person interview, Oslo, 28 June.

Fossbakken, Tore. 2017. Post Producer on *SKAM* and *blank* at NRK, in-person interview, Oslo, 29 November.

Furevold-Boland, Marianne. 2016. Project Leader on *SKAM* at NRK, in-person interview, Oslo, 13 December.

Game of Thrones. HBO. 2011–2019.

Grainge, Paul, and Catherine Johnson. 2015. *Promotional Screen Industries*. London and New York: Routledge.

Gray, Jonathan. 2003. New Audiences, New Textualities: Anti-fans and Non-fans. *International Journal of Cultural Studies* 6 (1): 64–81.

———. 2010. *Show Sold Separately. Promos, Spoilers, and Other Media Paratexts*. New York: New York University Press.

Greene, Andy. 2013. How 'Lilyhammer' Changed the TV World. *Rolling Stone*, 5 December.

Gulliksen, Hildri. 2017. Head of NRK Super, in-person interview, Oslo, 19 May.

Hale, Mike. 2012. From Netflix and Norway, a Wiseguy in Not-Quite-Paradise. *The New York Times*, 5 February.

Hammett-Jamart, Julia, Petar Mitric, and Eva Novrup Redvall, eds. 2018. *European Film and Television Co-production: Policy and Practices*. London and New York: Palgrave Macmillan.

Hansen, Magne. 2013. *Lilyhammer* solgt til over 130 Land. *NRK.no*, 15 February.

Hedemann, Ole. 2017. Head of International Formats at NRK, in-person interview, Oslo, 10 November.

———. 2018. *TV-formater. Fra Kvitt eller dobbelt til Skam*. Oslo: Cappelen Damm Akademiske.

Hegnsvad, Kristoffer. 2016. Verdens bedste ungdomsserie er norsk. *Politiken*, 25 August.

Helsingen, Arne. 2015. Head of Television at NRK, in-person interview, Oslo, 16 January.

Hill, Annette. 2019. *Media Experiences. Engaging with Drama and Reality Television*. London and New York: Routledge.

Hills, Matt. 2004. Rethinking Cult-TV: Texts, Inter-texts, and Fan Audiences. In *The Television Studies Reader*, eds. Robert C. Allen and Annette Hills. London: Routledge.

Hills, Matt, Michele Hilmes, and Roberta Pearson, eds. 2019. *Transatlantic Television Drama. Industries, Programmes, & Fans*. Oxford: Oxford University Press.

Hole, Åse Marie. 2017. Project Leader on *blank* at NRK, in-person interview, Oslo, 29 September.

Hoskins, Colin, and Stuart McFadyen. 1993. Canadian Participation in International Co-Productions and Co-Ventures in Television Programming. *Canadian Journal of Communication* 18 (2): 219–236.

House of Cards. 2013–2018. Netflix.

Hughes, Sarah. 2016. Shame: A Scandi TV Sensation for the Social Media Generation. *The Guardian*, 4 December.

Jacobsen, Ushma Chauhan, and Pia Majbritt Jensen. 2020. Unfolding the Global Travel of Danish Television Drama Series. In *The Global Audiences of Danish Television Drama*, eds. Pia Majbritt Jensen and Ushma Chauhan Jacobsen, 9–19. Göteborg: Nordicom.

Jenkins, Henry. 2006. *Convergence Culture. Where Old and New Media Collide*. New York and London: New York University Press.

Jenter/Girls. NRK. 2013–2018.

Jerslev, Anne. 2017. SKAM's 'lige her' og 'lige nu'. Om *SKAM* og nærvær. *Nordisk Tidsskrift for Informationsvidenskab og kulturformidling* 62 (2): 75–81.

Krüger, Steffen, and Gry C. Rustad. 2019. Coping with Shame in a Media-Saturated Society: Norwegian Web Series *SKAM* as Transitional Object. *Television & New Media* 20 (1): 72–95.

Lang-Ree, Kari Anne. 2017. In-house Lawyer at NRK, in-person interview, Oslo, 27 October.

Lentz, Marianne. 2017. Skaberen af 'Skam': Jeg gennemlever alle de følelser, jeg udsætter mine karakterer for. DR.dk, 7 April.

LikMeg/LikeMe. NRK. 2018–present.

Lilyhammer. Rubicon TV for NRK and Netflix. 2012–2014.

Lindtner, Synnøve Skarsbø, and John Magnus Dahl. 2019. Aligning Adolescent to the Public Sphere: The Teen Serial *Skam* and Democratic Aesthetic. *Javnost— the Public* 26 (1): 54–69.

Lobato, Ramon. 2019. *Netflix Nations. The Geography of Digital Distribution.* New York: New York University Press.

Lovleg/Legal. Rubicon TV for NRK. 2018–2019.

Lund, Øyvind. 2015. Head of Media at NRK, in-person interview, Oslo, 4 February.

Magnus, Mari. 2016. *SKAM* – når fiksjon og virkelighet møtes. *Nordicom Information* 38 (2): 31–38.

———. 2017. Online Producer on *SKAM*, in-person interview, Oslo, 12 January.

Maurud, Johan Hveem. 2018. Actor on *blank* at NRK, in-person interview, Oslo, 28 June.

Max, D.T. 2018. *SKAM*, the Radical Teen Drama that Unfolds One Post at a Time. *New Yorker*, 18 June.

McDermott, Patrick D.. 2017. Why The Whole Planet is Obsessed with This Norwegian Teen Drama. *The Fader*, 10 April.

MIA. NRK. 2010–2012.

Mohr, Emil. 2018. Netflix-sjefen gir norske 'Lilyhammer' æren for internasjonal suksess. *Aftenposten*, 18 April.

Molstad, Ragnar. 2017. Photographer on *SKAM* (S3) and *blank* at NRK, in-person interview, Oslo, 21 December.

Moran, Albert, ed. 2010. *TV Formats Worldwide: Localising Global Programs.* Chicago: Chicago University Press.

Næsheim, Knut. 2017. Director and Writer (Showrunner) on *blank* at NRK, in-person interview, Oslo, 27 September.

NFI. 2018. The Golden Age of Norwegian TV Drama. No author.

Nordlie, Hege Gaarder. 2017. Assistant Scriptwriter on *blank* at NRK, in-person interview, Oslo, 6 December.

———. 2018. Assistant Scriptwriter on *blank* at NRK, in-person interview, Oslo, 28 June.

Nyborg, Ingvill Marie. 2012. *MIA* – et stort og stille drama på nett. *NRKBeta. no*, 3 May.

Nylander, Sara. 2017. *SKAM* mest tittade på SVT Play—någonsin. SVT.no, 14 January.

Oren, Tasha, and Sharon Shahaf, eds. 2012. *Global Television Formats: Understanding Television across Borders.* 1st ed. London and New York: Routledge.

Øverlie, Tom. 2017. Online Developer on *SKAM* and *blank* at NRK P3 Event and Development, in-person interview, Oslo, 5 December.

Perkins, Steven. 2017. All the Things that *Skam* Got Right. stevenperkins.word-press.com, 2 January.

Petersen, Line Nybro, and Vilde Schanke Sundet. 2019. Play Moods across the Life Course in *SKAM* Fandom. *Journal of Fandom Studies* 7 (2): 113–131.

Radish, Christina. 2013. Steven Van Zandt Talks *Lilyhammer*, Netflix's Original Programming, Living and Working in Norway, and What He Hopes Viewers Get from Watching the Show. *Collider.com*, 12 December.

Red Arrow. 2012. *Lilyhammer* Rating Information. Not dated. http://www.redarrowinternational.tv/fiction/series/dramedy/lilyhammer.php

Renaud, Jean-Luc, and Barry R. Litman. 1985. Changing Dynamics of the Overseas Marketplace for TV Programming: The Rise of International Co-Production. *Telecommunication Policy* 9 (3): 245–261.

Rønning, Tone C. 2015. Head of Drama at NRK External and Executive Producer on *Lilyhammer*, in-person interview, Oslo, 27 January.

Sara. NRK. 2008–2009.

Selznick, Barbara J. 2008. *Global Television: Co-Producing Culture*. Philadelphia: Temple University Press.

SKAM Austin. XIX Entertainment for Facebook Watch. 2018–2019.

SKAM Espania. Zeppelin TV for Movistar+. 2018–2020.

SKAM France. France Televisions for France tv slash. 2018–present.

SKAM Italia. TIMvision. 2018–present.

SKAM/SHAME. NRK. 2015–2017.

Skodvin, Eilif. 2015. Showrunner on *Lilyhammer* at Rubicon TV, in-person interview, Oslo, 18 February.

Sørensen, Håkon Lund. 2017. *SKAM* Statistic. Internal Document Given by E-mail, 17 February.

Sprus, Nathalie. 2018. NRK's Press Contact on *SKAM* and *blank* at NRK, in-person interview, Oslo, 19 February.

Straubhaar, Joseph D. 2007. *World Television: From Global to Local*. Los Angeles: Sage Publication.

Sundet, Vilde Schanke. 2016. Still 'Desperately Seeking the Audience'? Audience Making in the Age of Media Convergence (the *Lilyhammer* Experience). *Northern Lights* 14 (1): 11–27.

———. 2017a. Co-Produced Television Drama and the Cost of Transnational 'Success': The Making of *Lilyhammer*. In *Building Successful & Sustainable Film & Television Business: A Cross-National Perspective*, eds. Eva Bakøy, Roel Puijk, and Andrew Spicer, 67–88. Bristol: Intellect.

———. 2017b. 'Det er bare du som kan føle det du føler' – emosjonell investering og engasjement i nettdramaet *SKAM*. *16:9 Filmtidsskrift*.

———. 2019. From Secret Online Teen Drama to International Cult Phenomenon: The Global Expansion of *SKAM* and its Public Service Mission. *Critical Studies in Television* 15 (1): 69-90.

———. 2020a. Drama as Flagship Productions: Small Nations Television and Digital Distribution. In *Danish Television Drama: Global Lessons from a Small Nation*, eds. Anne Marit Waade, Eva Novrup Redvall, and Pia Majbritt Jensen, 147–165. Palgrave Macmillan.

————. 2020b. 'Will it Translate?'—SKAM som remake. In *Streaming for vidrekomne*, eds. Jacob Isak Nielsen, Andreas Halskov, and Henrik Højer, 68–89. Tubine.

Sundet, Vilde Schanke, and Line Nybro Petersen. 2020. Ins and Outs of Transmedia Fandom: Motives for Entering and Exiting the *SKAM* Fan Community Online. *Poetics*. Online first. https://doi.org/10.1016/j.poetic.2020.101510.

The Crown. 2016–present. Netflix.

The Office. 2001–2003. BBC.

Waisbord, Silvio. 2007. McTV: Understanding the Global Popularity of Television Formats. In *Television. The Critical View. Seventh Edition*, ed. Horace Newcomb, 375–396. New York and Oxford: Oxford University Press.

Wallace, Petter. 2015. Head of External Productions at NRK, in-person interview, Oslo, 15 January.

Weissmann, Elke. 2012. *Transnational Television Drama: Special Relations and Mutual Influence between the US and UK*. New York: Palgrave Macmillan.

Wisløff, Anne. 2018. Showrunner on *Sara, Mia, Jenter, LikMeg* at NRK Super, in-person interview, Oslo, 9 March.

Woldsdal, Nicolay, and Ingunn Michelsen. 2016. *Skam* slår alle rekorder. *NRK.no*, 21 December.

WtFOCK. Sputnik Media for VIER. 2018–present.

CHAPTER 4

Changing Publishing Strategies

Abstract This chapter discusses how streaming impacts *television publishing*—that is, how online and on-demand television contest the traditional publishing strategies of linear 'flow' television, and how the industry responds by developing new ways to present, contextualise and distribute drama content. This chapter is organised according to three key publishing strategies for television drama: to *reinvent 'flow' and 'liveness'*, to create *transmedia universes* and to present *events*. This chapter demonstrates how these publishing strategies increasingly explore new ways of telling stories, and distribute and promote drama series, while adding layers of meaning for the audience to explore. This chapter uses *Lilyhammer*, *SKAM* and *blank* to illustrate the key tendencies and arguments.

Keywords Event • Liveness • Publishing models • Streaming • Television drama • Transmedia

INTRODUCTION

How does streaming affect the *publishing* of television drama, and what types of publishing strategies does streaming favour in particular? Following upon my earlier reviews of industry perceptions of streaming (Chap. 2) and new production cultures (Chap. 3), this chapter addresses the specific ways in which online and on-demand television contest the

© The Author(s), under exclusive license to Springer Nature
Switzerland AG 2021
V. S. Sundet, *Television Drama in the Age of Streaming*,
https://doi.org/10.1007/978-3-030-66418-3_4

traditional publishing strategies of linear 'flow' television and the industry response—to develop new ways of presenting, contextualising and distributing drama content. The term 'publishing' builds on Bernard Miége's (1989) work on cultural industry logics, later developed by David Hesmondhalgh (2007) and Amanda D. Lotz (2017). Miége organises media production into three models—the publishing model, the flow model and the written model—and centres each model in different industries (films, books and music in the publishing model; radio and television in the flow model; newspaper and magazines in the written model) with different logics. For instance, Miége describes how the publishing model is characterised by 'cultural commodities composed of isolated individual works' (1989: 144), while the flow model is characterised by a continuous flow of goods where the main activity is to schedule the flow. As argued by Lotz (2017: 19), streaming and internet-distributed television remove television from the characteristics of the flow model and bring it closer to the publishing model.

In this chapter, I highlight three publishing strategies, in particular. First, *publishing strategies aiming to reinvent 'flow' and 'liveness'*, meaning that they work with some aspect of time in television consumption, either by allowing the audience to decide when (and where) to watch drama series or by introducing a 'timer' for when to watch, thus reinstating a formal schedule of sorts. Examples of these respective alternatives include *Lilyhammer*'s binge-publishing strategy and *SKAM*'s (and *blank*'s) real-time publishing strategy. Second, *publishing strategies aiming to create transmedia narratives and universes*, meaning that they work with some aspect of place in both storytelling and television consumption. These strategies typically use multiple texts to create a 'coherent narrative world' (Evans 2011: 173), wherein 'each medium does what it does best' (Jenkins 2006: 96, 108–113) and where the audience can take part in the process as well. The transmedia story worlds of *SKAM* and *blank* are presented as examples. Other well-known examples include *Lost* (ABC, 2004–2010), *The Matrix* (Warner Bros., 1990) and *Doctor Who* (BBC, 1963–1969, 2005–present). Third, *publishing strategies aiming to present television as an event*, meaning that they not only try to attract an audience across time and place but also want to create a feeling of something which is out of the ordinary. Again, *SKAM* will exemplify several types of related events, ranging from specific programmes and campaigns to the cultivation of the general understanding that *SKAM*—and real-time online drama in general—represents a continuous (global) 'live' event while on air.[1]

This chapter argues that streaming accommodates some publishing strategies better than others. These strategies answer to the challenge of achieving greater visibility and exposure, as described in Chap. 2, and respond to the fear that 'you can have world-class content, and there is still a chance that no one would discover it' (Eriksen interviewed 2019). A key premise is that promotion and contextualisation are becoming increasingly important in a streaming television market and that both inform successful publishing strategies. Promotion and buzz, that is, attract the audience to drama series in the first place, while contextualisation sets the audience's expectations towards these series. In developing my arguments, I build on Jonathan Gray's (2010) work on 'paratexts', or texts that prepare us for other texts by shaping our expectations and 'reading strategies' (2010: 25; see also Genette 2001 [1997]).[2] Gray distinguishes between two types of paratexts: 'entryway paratexts', which try to control the viewer's entrance into and expectations of the text *beforehand* (e.g. watching a television promo before seeing the show), and 'in medias res paratexts', which the viewer encounters *after* entering the text but which still guides the viewer's reading of it (for instance, reading a review after seeing a show) (2010: chapter 2). According to Gray, no text exists without paratexts, which can be either industry produced or audience created. For example, Gray notes that fan creativity serves as 'a powerful in medias res paratext, grabbing a story or a text in midstream and directing its path

---

[1] This chapter uses *Lilyhammer*, *SKAM* and *blank* to discuss recent publishing trends. The publishing models of *Lilyhammer* and *SKAM* are also discussed in earlier publications, most importantly Sundet 2016 (*Still 'Desperately seeking the audience'? Audience making in the age of media convergence (the Lilyhammer experience)*) and Sundet 2019 (*From 'secret' online teen drama to international cult phenomenon: The global expansion of SKAM and its public service mission*). This chapter also draws on an interview study with fifty Scandinavian *SKAM*-fans from thirteen to seventy years old, conducted in collaboration with Line Nybro Petersen (see Chap. 1). This study is also reported in earlier publications, most importantly Petersen and Sundet 2019 (*Play moods across the life course in SKAM fandom*) and Sundet and Petersen 2020 (*Ins and outs of fandom: Motives for entering and exiting the SKAM fan community online*).

[2] The term 'paratext' is drawn from literary theory, where it describes the way in which novels are framed by the texts that surround them, including book cover copy, forewords and author interviews (Genette 2001 [1997]). Gray writes, 'Paratexts condition our entrance to texts, telling us what to expect, and setting the terms of our "faith" in subsequent transubstantiation. (…) Each paratext acts like an airlock to acclimatize us to a certain text, and it demands or suggests certain reading strategies' (2010: 25).

elsewhere, or forcing the text to fork outwards in multiple directions' (2010: 146). Any study of paratext, Gray argues, is therefore 'a study of how meaning is created, and of how texts begin' (2010: 26)—no text is ever 'finished', then, because it is continuously informed by both entryway and in media res paratexts. These lines of thoughts fit well with Annette Hill's (2019) concept of 'roaming audiences' and audience as 'pathmakers'. Essential to these terms are that audiences take different pathways and trace through the media landscape, leaving them with different experiences, but also that these paths are created by the television industry, other media, *and* audiences and fans themselves (see also Chaps. 3 and 5). By contextualising the three publishing strategies using the theory of paratextuality and the perspective of a roaming audience, this chapter demonstrates how they blur the lines between storytelling, distribution and promotion, adding new layers of meaning for the audience to explore across both time and space (see also Grainge and Johnson 2015).

Reinventing 'Flow' and 'Liveness'

The first publishing strategy involves *reinventing 'flow' and 'liveness'*, highlighting aspects of time and temporality in television consumption. In linear television, programmes are scheduled in predefined slots on particular channels to match the audience they are intended to attract. Traditional scheduling is based on rigid and predetermined time intervals dictating a rhythm of consumption categorised by regular intervals. Studies have demonstrated the importance of a good schedule in creating a continuous flow—that is, an ongoing stream of images and sounds designed to stabilise viewing habits over time. For Raymond Williams (2005 [1974]), flow captured how the television experience is planned as sequences of programmes, where audiences are 'watching television' rather than watching programmes. Techniques for doing so include both vertical and horizontal programming, the first to create flow during the day, and the second to create it during the week (for a historical account of this strategy, see Gitlin 1983). Studies have also demonstrated the importance of scheduling for contextualising television programmes, as both slots and channels indicate to the audience what to expect and therefore serve as vital entryway paratexts (Gray 2010; see also Ellis 2000; Ihlebæk et al. 2014).

Television streaming contests these principles, however, because programmes are not pre-scheduled on a particular channel or at a particular time but instead made available through a searchable portal where the viewer can choose what, when and where to watch. As such, the power of choice shifts increasingly to the audience rather than the broadcasters (Lotz 2009, 2017; see also Chap. 2). Consequently, television providers need ways beyond horizontal and vertical programming to attract viewers, create flow and restabilise viewing habits. Related strategic initiatives include both attractive and exclusive ('going big') productions, and relevant and niche ('going small') productions, as described elsewhere, as well as algorithmic recommendations based on viewers' previous preferences. For public service broadcasters, however, such recommendations must respond to the notion of public service itself by encompassing both important *and* popular titles, thus giving the audience both what they want and what they (presumably) need (Van den Bulck and Moe 2017).

A growing corpus of literature addresses algorithmic recommendations and new scheduling techniques for online and streaming television (see Bruun 2020: chapter 2 for a useful overview; see also Johnson 2019). According to Hanne Bruun (2020), however, we should not consider linear and non-linear television paradigms to be mutually exclusive; instead, they coexist and inform one another (2020: chapter 7). While Bruun acknowledges that you can now watch an episode of a drama series 'on your phone while sitting on the train to work', thriving scheduling practices continue to indicate that 'the majority of television consumption is still taking place in the private sphere, e.g., the home, and in the leisure time even if the content is accessed from a multitude of devices' (2020: 110). This *duality of consumption* of linear and non-linear television depending on the content, context and mood was very familiar to many NRK informants. To start with, they were quick to recognise how using several publishing platforms and strategies *together* would benefit NRK's content the most, in terms of both building awareness of NRK's overall catalogue and providing audience choice concerning specific titles. This notion also informs the abiding interest in *flexible* content rights, as described in Chap. 2. NRK's Head of Television summarised the situation as follows: 'Linear channels build on-demand use, and I think on-demand use also builds back on the linear channels' (Helsingen interviewed 2015). Many of the informants forecast the ultimate dominance of streaming but, until that time, saw the need to plan for both modes.

Lessons from both *Lilyhammer* and *SKAM* informed these strategies as well. In the case of the former, NRK revisited binge-publishing, as described in Chap. 3. As one informant noted, 'We have registered that streaming and binge-watching are ways people watch television' (Flesjø interviewed 2015). *Lilyhammer* was not the first series NRK applied binge-publishing on. For instance, in 2013, NRK binge-publish an NRK children series, and it became a huge streaming success (NRK 2013). Nevertheless, Netflix's use of binge-watching as its main publishing strategy spurred NRK's work on the topic and made it a more pressing issue. Consequently, *Lilyhammer* season 3 was the first high-profile, prime-time television drama to which NRK applied the 'all-you-can-eat' model.

The binge-publishing of *Lilyhammer* had mixed results for NRK, however. In general, season 3 had lower audience ratings than the previous two seasons on both linear and on-demand channels.[3] Hence, at the time, *Lilyhammer* did not convince NRK of the binge-publishing model's superiority, at least in terms of boosting audience numbers. Furthermore, ratings showed that relatively few viewers binge-watched the whole of season 3, and many on-demand viewers stuck to the linear schedule even though the episodes were all available online. In short, viewers were increasingly watching *Lilyhammer* at their own pace but continued to abide by the weekly schedule and turned to on-demand mostly to catch up (see Figs. 4.1 and 4.2). For many NRK informants, *Lilyhammer* therefore demonstrated the continuing duality of consumption and the close relationship between linear and on-demand channels. *Lilyhammer* also proved the overall power of television to represent an arena for 'imaginary communities' (Anderson 1991 [1983]) and shared experiences. As NRK's Head of Drama noted a few years later, 'We believe people need a community—to feel that they are part of something bigger' (Køhn interviewed 2017). NRK's Broadcasting Director also said the same: 'Today, we aim to be a public arena. We must build it through several instruments and channels' (Eriksen interviewed 2019; see also Chap. 2). Annette Hill (2019) identifies similar findings in her audience study of *Broen/The Bridge* (SVT/DR, 2011–2018). Here, she finds the transnational audiences of the show to use streaming for catch up before tuning into watching in a linear manner each Sunday. She also describes how young viewers express a sense of relief not having to plough through all the episodes at once in Netflix-style, and referring to the once-a-week watching as giving them

---

[3] On the linear channel, season 3 had an average market share of 30 per cent, compared to 47 per cent in season 2 and 55 per cent in season 1 (Tolonen 2015: 3). Regarding on-demand consumption, the audience figures for season 3 were lower than the two previous ones: season 3 had, on average, 850,000 views, compared to over 1 million views in season 2 (Tolonen 2015: 46).

the 'experience of old television', that is, 'a retro television experience when audiences assembled themselves in order to enjoy drama as a social ritual' (2019: 188).

Figures 4.1 and 4.2 illustrate *Lilyhammer*'s web rating week for week for seasons 2 and 3, respectively, showing how online viewers also in

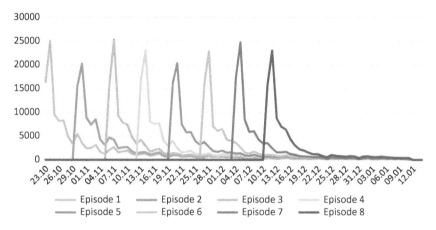

Fig. 4.1   *Lilyhammer*'s daily web rating on NRK TV (online player), season 2

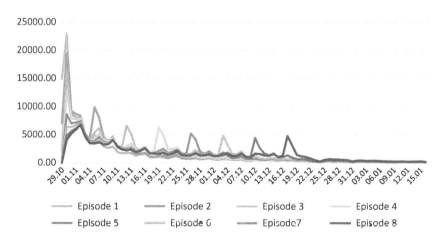

Fig. 4.2   *Lilyhammer*'s daily web rating on NRK TV (online player), season 3

season 3 followed a weekly schedule defined by linear television even though all the episodes were available for binging on NRK's online player. (Source: Tolonen (2015: 17))

As many informants were eager to point out, binge-publishing had many opportunities and benefits. It gave the audience greater control of when, where and what to consume, and some noted that it enabled more complex storylines because the audience no longer ran the risk of missing an episode in the middle of the season: 'There is no doubt we can have more complex plots and characters in drama productions when they are not consumed weekly. (…) I think we have only seen the beginning of how this will affect drama production' (Wallace interviewed 2015; see also Lotz 2007). Furthermore, in the time that followed *Lilyhammer*, NRK brought out several other shows they defined as streaming or binge-publishing successes, which promoted the publishing model (see, for instance, Andersen 2019; Helle 2019; Pedersen 2019; Woldsdal and Michelsen 2016). At the same time, however, binge-publishing encouraged the sort of personalised consumption which contested both NRK's and, presumably, the audience's need to partake in a larger community. As such, the binge-publishing model ran the risk of burying good content in a larger portfolio and fragmenting audience consumption.

The real-time publishing model of *SKAM* and *blank* (and real-time online drama more generally), on the other hand, developed an ongoing momentum for these shows by providing the audience with a continuity different from that of either linear or non-linear consumption. As already described, the real-time format of these series made their publishing rhythm irregular, unpredictable and addictive. *SKAM*'s Online Producer explained, 'The characters and their stories decide when we publish' (Magnus interviewed 2017). Another informant observed, 'To hold back—to do the exact opposite of what you do in any other television show you "binge" during the weekend—works in online drama' (Øverlie interviewed 2017). This publishing model compelled the audience to check back frequently for updates, as they never knew when a new update would come. As one fan explained, 'The small drops make you think about the show the whole week. It stays on the top of your mind. (…) It is a genius way to get people hooked' (Man 40, interviewed 2017). This sentiment echoes findings from fan studies, showing how uncertainty can be a pleasurable part of the viewing process (Pearson 2010). Similarly, Matt Hills (2018) uses the term 'always-on fandom' to describe the everyday digital experience of being a fan today, observing that waiting builds community around a production. Or as Billy Ehn and Orvar Löfgren (2010) note, from an 'emotional perspective, waiting conceals something more dramatic than just doing nothing' (2010: 66).

Consequently, online drama played with a sense of *live storytelling* and made audience members feel like they were watching an ongoing experience (Magnus 2016). Furthermore, it generated a sense of simultaneity and 'liveness' as the characters' lives unfolded in parallel with their target audiences, which created a new schedule of sort (Jerslev 2017; Sundet 2017). As stressed by one informant overlooking the development of online dramas in NRK Super, 'to create the feeling of simultaneous lives' (Gulliksen interviewed 2017) had been core to online drama since the beginning. As she further explained, 'the idea was for the audience to follow a girl in the same age as them living the same life as them—just a bit more tension saturate—day by day in real-time' (Gulliksen interviewed 2017). Or as formulated by *blank*'s Showrunner, heading for youths instead of teens, 'if you wake up with a hangover when the main character has a hangover or get a clip from school when you are at school, the real-time potential is completely fulfilled' (Næsheim interviewed 2017).

Figure 4.3 illustrates *SKAM*'s real-time publishing strategy during one week in season 3 (October 29 to November 10, 2016), showing how video clips, chat messages and Instagram pictures were dropped at various times on the blog (skam.p3.no) during the week. Audience never knew in beforehand when the next update would appear or what form it would take.

The term 'liveness' is often used theoretically to describe the way in which 'live television seeks to present itself as something natural and

Fig. 4.3 *SKAM* as a drama told in real-time ('live' storytelling), one week of season 3

immediately given' (Ytreberg 2009: 477)—that is, as an event which seems to unfold via an immediate, 'here-and-now' logic (Feuer 1983). Several scholars have also applied the term to online and digital platforms to describe how multiplatform formats such as *Big Brother* and *Pop Idol* give viewers a sense of watching an instantaneous event and construct a 'temporal co-presence' with them (Ytreberg 2009: 479; see also Couldry 2002; Kjus 2009). Similarly, studies of K-pop fandoms have shown how the daily, mediated interaction between K-pop idols and their fans creates a powerful 'experience of liveness' (King-O'Riain 2020: 2) which intensifies these fans' emotions. 'Liveness' is useful to the analysis of real-time online drama as well, precisely because these series plays with a sense of continuity, liveness and temporal co-presence. They deliberately give the *impression of being live* without being transmitted as such—hence, they are 'liveness with a difference' (Ytreberg 2009: 478). Of course, real-time online drama also distinguishes itself from live television and multiplatform formats in that what it contains is not, in fact, 'real' but rather fictional storytelling presenting itself as 'so close to reality that it could be true' (Nyborg 2012). In fact, real-time publishing could be said to deliberately blur the lines between reality and fiction in order to increase its audience's identification with it (Magnus 2016). The term 'authenticity' is often applied to these series as well. It acknowledges both their closeness to realism and accurate, detailed representation of everyday life, and it recognises the immediacy which emerges from the way in which real-time publishing and social media content are used to script spontaneity and create a feeling of liveness and immediacy that goes beyond traditional television drama (Sundet 2019). As explained by one informant with experience at both *SKAM* and *blank*, 'these series aim to appear as real universes. We treat these fictional series as if they were real' (Sprus interviewed 2018; see also Jerslev 2017).

The strategy of using authenticity and realness to create a sense of liveness also helped NRK to promote these shows, which otherwise avoided traditional television promos, press packages and actor interviews (official paratexts) and instead relied upon word-of-mouth (audience-created paratexts). One informant explained, 'There is no teaser in online drama because it hasn't happened yet. (…) We try not to puncture the universe by talking about the production' (Sprus interviewed 2018). Keeping the actors away from the media spotlight was not only a way to protect them (Svendsen 2016) but also a means of lending authenticity to their fictional characters and the fictional universe they occupied: 'We are living *in* the universe', said one (Sprus interviewed 2018). This promotion strategy also encouraged 'teen ownership' (Faldalen 2016) of these series, as *SKAM's* Showrunner explained, 'We wanted them [teens] to spread the word among themselves, not in an adult world, but as something only they knew about' (Andem quoted in Faldalen 2016). Similarly, informants from *blank* talked about identifying youth 'ambassadors' within the target audience group, which could help distribute news about the show *without* using a broader promotion strategy or draw the attention of older audiences or the media (Melbø interviewed 2017).

The real-time publishing strategy even realised a sort of 'double liveness', in that fans were watching the characters' lives as they happened (and in parallel with their own lives) but also at the same time that other members of the audience were watching too (Sundet 2019: 10). Hence, *SKAM* and *blank* transcended traditional 'imaginary communities' in the way in which audience members engaged with one another in the comments section following every update, as well as on social media and even in real life, all in real-time (see also Sundet and Petersen 2020). One fan described *SKAM* as a show 'you could attend *while* it was happening' (Woman 48, interviewed 2017). Another said, 'You look forward to the clip, but you also look forward to discussing the clip—that is half the fun' (Woman 26, interviewed 2017). In sum, it created an extended sense of liveness. As a result, plots and peaks in the storyline can easily be traced from the daily or weekly audience charts. As Fig. 4.4 shows, more people tuned in when the suspense was increasing.

Figure 4.4 depicts weekly unique visitors on *SKAM's* website (seasons 1–4), illustrating how each season over time built tension increasing the numbers of viewers visiting the website weekly (Source: Sørensen (2019: 5)).[4]

The real-time publishing model set a timer for when to watch these shows but also when to *discuss* them. This dynamic fuelled fan engagement, as I will discuss in Chap. 5—fans were continually linked to these shows and one another on a daily basis during the seasons. Many would alert each other or the fan community when new updates dropped, then start discussions about the storyline. The publishing strategy both sustained existing viewers and attracted new ones by generating daily buzz

---

[4] Every season had a short 'break' (called 'black week') to give the production a few days to get ahead and to build anticipation in the audience; these breaks represented small drops in viewership in each of the four seasons. The peak between seasons 2 and 3 reflects the teaser of season 3, announcing Isak as the new main character.

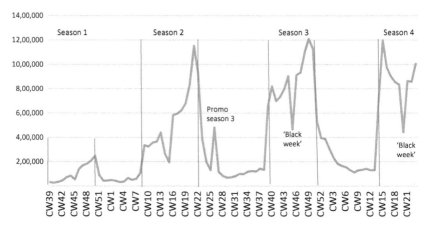

Fig. 4.4   Weekly unique visitors on *SKAM*'s website (skam.p3.no), seasons 1–4

about these shows, giving them *continuity* (see also Bourdon 2000). *SKAM*'s buzz was particularly effective at spreading the word, initially among Norwegian teens and later to international audiences, thanks to a massive number of fan-created paratexts concerning the show. The Danes were the first national audience outside Norway to discover *SKAM*, in the summer of 2016, before its popularity grew quickly in the autumn following the buzz related to season 3. During that third season, almost one-third of *SKAM*'s online viewers came from Denmark (Sørensen 2017a).[5]

Interestingly, some NRK informants saw *SKAM* and *blank* as arguments for a dual publishing strategy. The production teams and fans preferred these shows to be daily online drama series to be watched online and in real-time—and, as shown in Chap. 3, much work was done to make them fit this format. They were however also made available as weekly television episodes to be published on NRK's TV Player, and even its linear youth channel (NRK3), to accommodate more conventional viewing modes. This meant that the production teams had to produce these series to work both as real-time online dramas—told across multiple

---

[5] The numbers here include only measurable views on *SKAM*'s website, NRK's TV player and NRK's linear channels. They do not include views of fan-translated *SKAM* videos on Google-drive accounts, Dailymotion, YouTube or other social media commonly used by non-Norwegian-speaking viewers and fans.

platforms—*and* as regular television episodes. For viewers and fans, the two consumption modes differed and impacted the respective experiences, and in our fan study, we find a strong inclination towards watching in real-time. It was seen as the 'correct way' to watch, which also gave the most satisfaction to the viewer (Petersen and Sundet 2019; Sundet and Petersen 2020; see also Bengtsson et al. 2018). One fan recalled, 'It was completely different to "binge" *SKAM*, as I did in season 1 and 2, than it was to follow it in real-time and live with it from day to day, hour to hour—*being* the main character—as I did in season 3 and partly season 4' (Woman 48, interviewed 2017; see also Guttu 2016). For some fans, following a real-time drama could even be too absorbing, leaving little room for other activities: 'I almost found season 3 [of *SKAM*] bothersome because it was so intense. I almost looked forward to it ending, because I used so much time and effort thinking about *SKAM*' (Man 40, interviewed 2017). In any case, the mixed publishing strategy helps to explain why *SKAM* was so widely known and evidently made it into an event, as to be described below. In Norway, *SKAM* had an average of more than one million viewers per television episode (not including views on the *SKAM* website) for each of its three first seasons, out of a population of only five million people in all (Sørensen 2017b; see Fig. 4.5 for an overview of how audiences watched *SKAM* during season 3).[6]

Figure 4.5 depicts *SKAM*'s total screen rating (season 3), showing how the show was consumed in different manners; video clips on the websites (skam.p3.no), web rating through the online player (NRK TV) and viewing through NRK's linear channel (NRK3). Consumption measured for the period from October 1 to December 31, 2017. (Source: Sørensen (2019: 9))

In sum, both the binge and real-time publishing models provided NRK with new ways to reach a streaming audience. They served different consumption modes depending upon whether viewers wanted to consume a whole season in one night or live with it alongside their own lives for several months. Because both models strayed far from the standard weekly television schedule, these shows did not have to fill fixed time slots, providing their storytellers with greater flexibility in the total number of episodes and the episode lengths. For instance, in season 3, *SKAM* published 135 updates, 48 of which were video clips of one to fourteen minutes in

---

[6] Season 1 had 1.19 million viewers; season 2, 1.26 million viewers; season 3, 1.14 million viewers; and season 4, 0.53 million viewers (Sørensen 2017b).

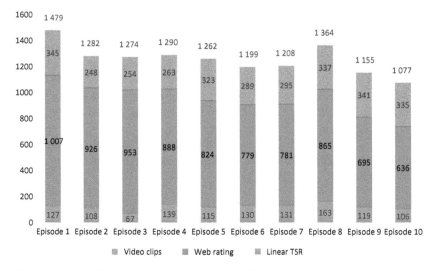

Fig. 4.5 *SKAM's* total screen rating (video clips, web rating and linear), season 3 (numbers in 1000)

length. This flexibility was appreciated by many. In the words of *blank*'s Assistant Scriptwriter: 'This is the way storytelling should be done; we should not have to fit an episode into a slot like a "straightjacket"—it can affect the quality of the storyline. Sometimes a story only needs sixteen, not thirty, minutes to be told' (Nordlie interviewed 2017).

Transmedia Storytelling and Universes

The second publishing strategy involves *creating transmedia narratives and universes*, meaning that it deals with the aspects of place and spatiality in storytelling and television consumption. Elizabeth Evans (2011) defines 'transmediality' as 'the increasingly popular industrial practice of using multiple media technologies to present information concerning a single fictional world through a range of textual forms' (2011: 1). She then distinguishes between 'transmedia storytelling' and 'transmedia distribution' (or engagement), the former referring to the integration of multiple texts to create a narrative so large that it cannot be contained by a single medium and the latter referring to the simultaneous (or near-simultaneous) distribution of content on multiple platforms (2011: 2). Real-time online drama belongs to the first category, as it aims to create a 'coherent narrative world' (Evans 2011: 173), where audience members are invited to be active participants and fans—being rewarded when investing time and effort in sharing, discussing and decoding the texts (see also Jenkins 2006). In the case of *SKAM* and *blank*, the chief platforms for the narrative were the websites (skam.p3.no, blank.p3.no), on which video clips, chat messages and pictures were published daily during a given season. Most of the key characters also had Instagram accounts—and some even had YouTube channels—which were used to extend the story world and lend authenticity and timeliness to the characters (Furevold-Boland interviewed 2016; Næsheim interviewed 2017).

According to Henry Jenkins (2006), transmedia storytelling is 'the art of world-making', wherein the audience takes on 'the roles of hunters and gatherers, chasing down bits of the story across media channels, comparing notes with each other', and audiences collaborate to 'ensure that everyone who invests time and effort will come away with a richer entertainment experience' (Jenkins 2006: 21). Seeing the audiences as 'hunters and gatherers' have similarities to Annette Hill's 'roaming audiences', where she defines the activity of roaming as 'one where people traverse the media landscape, following pathways and becoming pathfinders themselves' (2019: 11). In *SKAM* and *blank*, for example, participatory activities were embedded in the story world via the comment sections which followed updates on the websites, creating an extended paratextual universe of their own. *SKAM*'s four seasons generated close to 140,000 approved comments and more than 5,300,000 likes in all (Erlandsen 2018), demonstrating its fandom's significant engagement (see also Skarstein 2018). As described in Chap. 3, these comment sections had value for the production teams in terms of their continuous feedback as to how the audience was receiving the storyline and wanted it to proceed. However, the comment sections had value for the audience as well, by providing a platform for any viewer to share thoughts and emotions (see also Lindtner and Dahl 2019). They generated a strong contextual paratext around every show update, adding meaning, value and interpretations. They also functioned as mirrors of the viewers' feelings and emotions in the testimony of others (see also Sundet 2017; Sundet and Petersen 2020). Several studies address the emotional investment of fans (Hills 2002; Jenkins 1992; Jensen 1992) and the way in which an interest in sharing these emotions propels the creation of fan spaces (Cavicchi 1998; Harrington and Bielby 1995). For example, Kristina Busse (2018) uses the term 'love feedback loop' to describe how fan activities and collective actions feed the love fans already have: 'At its best, fandom is a love feedback loop that in turn generates more love, more fannish discussions, more fannish creations' (2018: 211).

The fact that these shows invited audience members and fans to follow their characters on social media as well—where they appeared authentic and even 'real'—strengthened the audience's identification with them and blurred the line between reality and fiction even more (Magnus 2016). As one informant explained, 'I think it's as simple as the feeling that this is happening here and now with someone you care about' (Erlandsen interviewed 2017). Or as another said, 'You know intellectually that this is not real, but you want to feel and think that it is' (Bettvik interviewed 2017). Many fans described the characters as people they 'checked in on' every day, and some even described them as close friends. These quotes echo findings from previous studies on 'parasocial relationship' (Horton and Wohl 1956), which describe how viewers can create connections and feelings towards television characters and experience them as close friends, even though the relationship is based on simulated interactions (see also Todd 2011). Viewers knew these relationships are imaginary, yet they are emotionally meaningful anyway (see also Williams 2015). For instance, when commenting on the blog, several fans would refer to the characters by name as though they were real people:

> Dear Even [love interest in *SKAM* season 3]. We have not heard from you in two days. We are worried and don't know where you are. Please come back, we can't sleep. Let Isak [main character in *SKAM* season 3] know you are okay, and everything will be fine. We miss you. Please come back. Best regards, the entire population of Norway (in addition to parts of the population of other countries). (Posted on *SKAM*'s blog, 01.11.2016, my translation)

Such a strong fan-character bond was precisely what the production team wanted for the show, and producers actively used social media accounts as intermediaries between the fictional universe and the audience to enhance this identification (Magnus 2016). Just as previous studies have shown how reality formats such as *Big Brother* and *Pop Idol* use digital and social media to create 'junction points' between platforms to 'highlight immediacy and involvement' (Ytreberg 2009: 476, 467), digital and social media fill similar functions in online drama formats as well. In short, these transmedia story worlds spread across platforms, but they were also interlinked temporarily by characters' online authenticity and the real-time publishing model, which together created narrative and temporal coherence across.

SKAM and *blank* were also produced as example of 'hyperdiegesis', which Matt Hills (2002) defines as 'the creation of a vast and detailed narrative space, only a fraction of which is ever directly seen or encountered within the text' (137). These shows presented fictional worlds which the audience experienced only in glimpses, though more information was always available if fans were willing to seek it out across platforms. While 'hyperdiegetic' generally describes cult texts with far more comprehensive narratives than either *SKAM* or *blank*, I defend its relevance here as well (Sundet 2019), as these transmedia worlds both played out in real-time *and* created a temporal complexity for the audience to explore. *SKAM*'s transmedia narrative also expanded even further with the *SKAM* remakes, which many fans took to be part of the larger whole as they sought parallels and intertextual references across shows.

In addition to the official transmedia story world created by the production teams—on the blog, Instagram and YouTube—these series also generated large fan-produced extensions of their universe via paratexts on the fans' own digital and social media platforms. For instance, fans created fan groups and fan accounts on Facebook and Tumblr, provided fan-driven character accounts on Instagram and Twitter, and produced fan art or wrote fan fiction. In the case of *SKAM*, more than 6000 fan fictions have been posted on the fan-provided platform *Archive of our own* alone, and the number goes up if one includes fan fiction concerning the *SKAM* remakes. As one fan said, 'something is always happening—on the blog, on Facebook, in a chat, or wherever you may be' (Woman 38, interviewed 2017; see also Sundet and Petersen 2020). This expansion of the show's universe—and the participatory activities enabled by these various social media platforms— helped to fill the time between show updates and sustained the immersive experience. The *SKAM* universe was even extended by commercial interests selling merchandise adorned with *SKAM* slogans and using *SKAM* in advertising as an intertextual reference (see Figs. 4.6 and 4.7).

Figures 4.6 and 4.7 illustrate *SKAM* as a transmedia universe extended by fans on social media (screenshot from @skametdukkehjem and @elli_ skam on Instagram) and by commercial interests in marketing, using the well-known *SKAM* brand, quotes from the series or pictures in their campaigns. The SAS and McDonald's ads are both actual commercials, but the Levi's ad is fan created, showing what one fan *wanted* should be an ad for Levi's.

Fig. 4.6   *SKAM* as a transmedia universe expanded by fans

Fig. 4.7   *SKAM* as a transmedia universe expanded by commercial interests

In sum, creating a transmedia narrative allows producers to tell a story in new and expanded ways while embedding audiences and fans deeper in the story world, spurring affection, identification and loyalty (see also Grossberg 1992; Hills 2002; Jenkins 1992; Sandvoss 2005). Transmediality also represents an efficient means of promoting content, as many fan scholars have discussed (see, for instance, Jenkins 2006). Both *blank* and *SKAM* used transmediality to engage the audience as fans, but, unlike some other transmedia franchises, not as *consumers*—they had nothing more than the shows themselves to 'sell'. NRK worked hard, in fact, to keep *SKAM* a non-commercial universe, despite the overwhelming commercial interest in the strong hype and positive paratextuality surrounding the show. NRK's in-house lawyer dealt with this issue: '*SKAM* is a show we made to give our audience high-quality content; it is not a commercial brand, and to keep it as non-commercial as possible has been of key importance' (Lang-Ree interviewed 2017). Nevertheless, NRK was careful to distinguish between commercial and non-commercial (teens' and fans') investment in the universe; she continued, 'We have a completely different tolerance towards fans. (...) Fans inspired by *SKAM* and playing with the material are great. It's something else if someone does it to make money' (Lang-Ree interviewed 2017).

TELEVISION DRAMA AS EVENT

The final publishing strategy involves *creating television drama as an event.* It seeks to attract an audience across time and place but also in great numbers, thus creating the feeling of something out of the ordinary (see also Hepp and Couldry 2010; Kjus 2009; Ytreberg 2009). This approach to television drama builds on the concept of the 'media event' originally presented by Daniel Dayan and Elihu Katz (1994)—in which they define the media event as an 'interruption of routine'. Paddy Scannell sums up the theory of media event as the study of 'the aura of the extraordinary (...) which stands out from the ordinary, the humdrum and routine' (2014: 178). Television programmes designed to be events which lack origins or alignments *outside* of the media are not media events as such, according to Dayan and Katz's definition. Daniel J. Boorstin (1992) uses the term 'pseudo-events' to describe them, but this term implies an inherent critique of such programmes as too promotional in nature. Others have argued for more neutral terms; Espen Ytreberg (forthcoming) suggests 'media-generated events', while Anders Hepp and Nick Couldry (2010) suggest 'popular media events' instead:

> Popular media events break with the everyday but in a much more routine way, they do not monopolize the media coverage in total, but in a certain segment ('tabloid', 'boulevard'), they do not happen 'live' but in a continuous development (quite often also of marketing and branding), they are mostly organized by the media themselves not just as pre-planned but as completely commercialized, they are less celebratory and more pleasure-oriented, often they polarize and generate the attention of certain 'cultural segments' (scenes, youth cultures, etc.) where popular media events have an outstanding role. (Hepp and Couldry 2010: 8)

Taking digital and online media platforms into consideration as well, Yngvar Kjus (2009) introduces the term 'event media' to describe the specific type of television programme (typically an entertainment or reality show) which presents as an event programme and uses online media platforms to engage the audience in various ways. Such efforts create the *feeling* of an event but are created to serve the needs and interests of the industry—Ytreberg (2009) describes them as 'designed for eventfulness' and notes that they 'tend to reach their audience with a strong sense of the eventfulness surrounding them' (2009: 473, 474). Referring to programmes such as *Big Brother* and *Pop Idol*, both Kjus and Ytreberg highlight the link between eventfulness and audience participation and engagement. While the actual impact of audience participation on the show is often limited (e.g. by voting for a participant in *Pop Idol*), the important thing is that the audience *feels* like it is taking part (see also Sundet and Ytreberg 2009). Ytreberg (2009) insists, 'The event of participation is there to be felt like making a difference, like being part of the event in a more immediate sense than that allowed by the vicarious participation of broadcasting' (2009: 476)—it is about, he continues, the 'feeling of being noticed' (2009: 476). Relatedly, studies of digital fandoms, including K-pop fans, recognise the role of daily mediated interactions and the experience of liveness in creating emotional closeness between audiences and idols (King-O'Riain 2020). Our *SKAM* fan study showed the same. One fan described how the show's comment section gave her a feeling of entering a dialogue with the production team: 'It gives you a feeling of being seen—that they [the show's producers] notice what we do' (Woman 13, interviewed 2017). Another fan applauded *SKAM*'s Showrunner Julie Andem's use of fan fiction and fan art as reference points within the show: 'It's very cool. We feel very recognised when she does that' (Woman 21, interviewed 2017). Similar, many fans referred to the last episode of the last season, where the *SKAM* team incorporated fan comments from the blog—showing again how they aimed for a close relationship with their viewers.

While studies of 'event media' (or 'media-generated events') typically address reality and entertainment shows (Kjus 2009; Ytreberg 2009), the theory applies to television series as well; Matt Hills (2015), for example, frames the anniversary of *Doctor Who* as a case of 'eventification', or something more than hype alone (see also Booth 2016). Drawing upon Hills's work on unfolding drama events and Ytreberg and Kjus's work on eventfulness in multiplatform formats, I will devote the rest of this chapter to *SKAM*'s marshalling of events ranging from particular programmes (e.g. *SKAM* safari tours and fan conventions) and campaigns (e.g. #williammåsvare and the EVAK forever campaigns) to the general cultivation of the understanding that *SKAM* represents a continuous (global) 'live' event whenever it is on the air. Crucial to my argument is the realisation that the tendency towards eventification is driven by *both* industry logics and fan behaviour. Eventfulness cannot be achieved through a single television programme or a single television series alone. It needs a circuit of coordinated paratexts that spreads across different platforms and gives the impression that something out of the ordinary can be achieved. Media-generated events therefore typically involve a complex push–pull dynamic between producers and audiences, where both sides contribute in creating the feeling of a larger media phenomenon that expands across media and platforms.

The first way to understand *SKAM* as an event is through the many *activities sparked by the show*, which, for some viewers and fans, transformed it from something to watch into something to do. At minimum, reading and writing in the comment section acted as a 'daily event' for many fans, but fans could also take part in *SKAM* parties or meet-ups. For instance, the Norwegian newspaper *Aftenposten* reported in 2017 on a Danish *SKAM* event where fans 'meet to watch *SKAM* on a big screen, discuss the show and eat fish cakes', which sold out in less than ten minutes (Villumsen 2016). A fan from our study described a small group he was involved in: 'Suddenly, we became a group that had Christmas parties and get-togethers, even though we did not know each other from beforehand' (Man 44, interviewed 2017). News articles observed *SKAM* fans coming to Norway on *SKAM* 'safaris', visiting places from the show and, hopefully, meeting some of the actors (NTB 2017; Revheim and Kalajdzic 2017; see also Williams 2017). One international fan exulted on Tumblr after meeting *SKAM* actor Tarjei Sandvik Moe (Isak) after a play he was in. She describes how she was not able to speak as her entire body 'just shut down and i stood there frozen not saying anything bc i was literally having an out of body experience hfkjdhgi', before summarising the rest of the evening; 'Hands down best moment of my entire life!! (and then me and Ashley literally .. ran all around grunerlokka [place in Oslo] screaming, and got really fucking drunk on a roof and i passed out and had to go to hospital skgjhasfkljg but literally still the best weekend of ym entire life!!!!)' (posted on Tumblr, 28.05.2017, slang and misspellings in original). Several *SKAM* fans took part in fan conventions, which were built on seeing the actors in real life but also meeting other fans with a similar level of dedication (see also Aanstad 2017). One fan recalled, 'It was an experience so loaded with everything we had been talking about for the past few months, all the experiences we had and all the emotions we had invested in. (…) It was a *once-in-a-lifetime experience*' (Woman 33, interviewed 2017). Clearly, for her, the convention was a dramatic 'interruption of routine' (Dayan and Katz 1994).

A second way to understand *SKAM* as an event is through the many *campaigns associated with it*. One example is the industry-driven #williammåsvare-event, in which the production team for season 2 (following the relationship between main character Noora and her love interest, William) deliberately linked a fan-produced hashtag (#williammåsvare, translating as #williamneedstoanswer) with the show's real-time publishing model to generate suspense in the storyline (Where is William? Will he answer?). It created a national buzz concerning the fictional character's whereabouts. As explained by *SKAM*'s Online Producer, 'we wanted to create a joint moment (...) That Friday at 5 pm became almost a linear television moment because everyone turned in to watch the clip at the same time' (Magnus interviewed 2017). This buzz filled *SKAM*'s comment section and fan group discussions but also appeared in the national media. The Norwegian newspaper *VG* somewhat ironically tweeted that school exams would be postponed until William had answered (tweeted May 23, 2015; see also Graatrud 2016). The production team even broke the record of unique users per hour on the *SKAM* website by announcing beforehand on the hashtag when the audience could expect William to answer (Sørensen 2017a: 16; see also Magnus 2016). As recalled by one informant, 'when William did not answer Noora in season 2, the blog (skam.p3.no) was four times larger than the rest of NRK and by far the largest website in Norway, perhaps in Europe' (Erlandsen interviewed 2017).

Another example of a campaign taking the form of an event was the so-called EVAK forever campaign. It was initiated by a small number of particularly invested fans following the nomination of Even and Isak (the couple from season 3, often referred to as EVAK by the fans) in an *E! News* 2017 poll for 'TV's Top Couple'. The campaign generated so much activity that the *SKAM* couple won the poll by tallying more votes than other fan-favourite couples from British and US productions (Bricker 2017). Many of the fans we interviewed expressed their enjoyment of the daily voting and the feeling of taking part in something so big with other fans. The campaign organisers had an even more powerful experience as they put up daily statistics on the polls, produced and posted memes and gifs to 'call for votes', and motivated larger international fan groups on Facebook, Tumblr and Instagram to eventually win the poll. One fan recalled, 'It was one of the most fun periods ever' (Woman 52, interviewed 2017), and another added, 'EVAK-forever made me feel I was part of the fandom' (Woman 48, interviewed 2017; see also Petersen and Sundet 2019). The fact that a couple from a series which had not even aired in the United

States managed to outcompete well-established US teen productions such as *Teen Wolf* (MTV, 2011–2017) and *The Vampire Diaries* (CW, 2009–2011) was seen as an empowering 'victory' by *SKAM* fans: 'We were probably fewer fans than many of the other fandoms, but we were better organised and more dedicated' (Woman 48, interviewed 2017). Such initiatives and campaigns then became 'collective memories' (King 2001) within the fan group—shared reference points which played an important role in creating group solidarity, a sense of belonging and common norms and rules.

In addition to the various arrangements and campaigns described above, there was the general sense of *SKAM*—and real-time drama in general—as *an ongoing event while on the air*. *SKAM*'s Online Producer, for example, called every season 'a large event with immediate feedback' (Magnus interviewed 2017), and *SKAM*'s Showrunner explained her departure for *SKAM Austin* in a similar way on Instagram: '*SKAM* is not my show. All of us own *SKAM*. It is not just a drama series, it's an *event* and a *community* that all of you are part of and contribute to' (posted 10.11.2017, my use of italics). The constant onslaught of content from both the production team and fans on social media helped to sustain the sense of *SKAM* as an ongoing (global) 'live' event as well. As one reviewer put it, season 3 of *SKAM* became a 'collective enchantment' which could only be experienced once, there and then (Guttu 2016). Clearly, for many people, taking part in *SKAM* meant taking part in a live happening which escaped the everyday routine of their lives.

Figure 4.8 illustrates *SKAM* as a continuous global 'live' event across social media during one day in season 4 (June 7, 2017), created by both

| SKAM-bloggen | Twitter | Instagram | Facebook | Tumblr | YouTube |

Fig. 4.8 *SKAM* as a continuous global 'live' event

NRK and fans and spread across multiple media platforms. Screenshots from the *SKAM* blog (skam.p3.no), Twitter, Instagram, one Facebook fan group, Tumblr and YouTube.

Summing Up

This chapter has analysed how streaming impacts three particular publishing strategies of television drama—those aiming to reinvent 'flow' and 'liveness' through binge-watching and real-time publishing strategies, those aiming to create transmedia narratives and universes, and those aiming to create events. All three resonate with the challenge of visibility and exposure, as discussed in Chap. 2, and highlight the importance of promotion and contextualisation in drama distribution. They also shed light on the ways in which streaming and television distribution via online and digital platforms increasingly blur the lines between storytelling, distribution and promotion while adding layers of meaning for the audience to explore. Furthermore, these strategies highlight how television institutions are becoming increasingly co-dependent on audiences, paratexts and a changing set of platforms to spread and make sense of their drama content.

The three publishing strategies were all activated by international trends but translated and adjusted by the NRK to fit a Norwegian public service audience. As such, they show how even a small nation like the Norwegian can take part in a global media landscape and even present new publishing trends, by being innovative in its approach. These publishing trends also highlight the advantage of being a licence-funded public broadcaster, as NRK did not have to fit its publishing strategies to either advertising or subscription model. In its experimentation with both binge-publishing, real-time publishing, transmedia and events, NRK was free to follow what was best for the storyline and the audience, not for the business model or the company's profitability.

A key argument of this chapter has been that streaming favours some publishing strategies over others, implying that streaming also *disfavours* some publishing strategies. Two examples of disfavoured publishing strategies are tent-poling and the use of prime-time. Tent-poling works by scheduling new or weak shows around an appealing and robust show—the pole in the middle holds up the two weaker shows. It proves less efficient in an on-demand streaming context where audiences do not necessarily follow either a schedule or programme recommendations. Similarly, streaming seems to disfavour prime-time as a publishing strategy—that is, scheduling a block of particular attractive (often expensive) shows at the most attractive viewing time, the evening. Again, when the audience chose for themselves when to watch, publishing strategies following certain times during the day and night lose value, pointing to an increased focus on prime-*shows* rather than prime-*times* (see also Chap. 3).

REFERENCES

Aanstad, Kristin Helle. 2017. *SKAM*-skuespillerne samlet igjen: - Vilde er det såreste i meg, og hun stiller alle spørsmålene jeg lurer på. *Aftenposten*, 21 September.

Andersen, Jacob. 2019. Herman Flesvik setter ny NRK-rekord – slår både *Exit* og *Parterapi*. *Kampanje.com*, 16 January.

Anderson, Benedict. 1991 [1983]. *Imagined Communities: Reflections on the Origin and Spread of Nationalism*. New York: Verso.

Bengtsson, Emilie, Rebecka Källquist, and Malin Sveningsson. 2018. Combining New and Old Viewing Practices: Uses and Experiences of the Transmedia Series *Skam*. *Nordicom Review* 39 (2): 63–77.

Bettvik, Ida. 2017. Production Leader on *SKAM* (S4) and *blank* at NRK, in-person interview, Oslo, 24 November.

blank. NRK. 2018–2019.

Boorstin, Daniel. 1992. *The Image: A Guide to Pseudo-events in America*. New York: Vintage Books.

Booth, Paul. 2016. *Crossing Fandoms*. Basingstoke: Palgrave Macmillan.

Bourdon, Jerome. 2000. Live Television is Still Alive: On Television as an Unfilled Promise. *Media, Culture & Society* 14 (4): 531–556.

Bricker, Tierney. 2017. TV's Top Couple 2017 Has a Winner and They're Thanking 'the Coolest Fanbase on Earth'. *EOnline*, 8 March.

Bruun, Hanne. 2020. *Re-Scheduling Television in the Digital Era*. London and New York: Routledge.

Busse, Kristina. 2018. Afterword. Fannish Affect and Its Aftermath. In *Everybody Hurts: Transitions, Endings, and Resurrections in Fan Cultures*, ed. Rebecca Williams, 209–218. Iowa City: University of Iowa Press.

Cavicchi, Daniel. 1998. *Tramps Like Us: Music and Meaning among Springsteen Fans*. New York: Oxford University Press.

Couldry, Nick. 2002. Playing for Celebrity. Big Brother as Ritual Event. *Television & New Media* 3 (3): 283–293.

Dayan, Daniel, and Elihu Katz. 1994. *Media Events: The Live Broadcasting of History*. Cambridge, MA: Harvard University Press.

Doctor Who. BBC. 1963–1989, 2005–present.

Ehn, Billy, and Orvar Löfgren. 2010. *The Secret World of Doing Nothing*. Berkeley, CA: University of California Press.

Ellis, John. 2000. Scheduling: The Last Creative Act in Television? *Media, Culture & Society* 22 (1): 25–38.

Eriksen, Thor Germund. 2019. Broadcasting Director at NRK, in-person interview, Oslo, 14 March.

Erlandsen, Kim. 2017. Online Developer on *SKAM* and *blank* at NRK P3 Event and Development, in-person interview, Oslo, 30 November.

———. 2018. SKAM Statistic—Likes and Comments on Blog. Information Given in a Meeting at the NRK, Oslo, Norway, 21 March.

Evans, Elizabeth. 2011. *Transmedia Television*. New York: Routledge.

Faldalen, Jon Inge. 2016. -Nerven i 'Skam' skal være sterk og relevant. *Rushprint. no*, 4 April.

Feuer, Jane. 1983. The Concept of 'Live Television': Ontology as Ideology. In *Regarding Television: Critical Approaches*, ed. E. Ann Kaplan, 12–22. Los Angeles: American Film Institute.

Flesjø, Nicolay. 2015. Editorial Director of On-Demand Services at NRK, in-person interview, Oslo, 26 January.

Furevold-Boland, Marianne. 2016. Project Leader on *SKAM* at NRK, in-person interview, Oslo, 13 December.

Genette, Gerard. 2001 [1997]. *Paratexts. Thresholds of Interpretation*. Cambridge: Cambridge University Press.

Gitlin, Tom. 1983. *Inside Prime Time*. New York: Pantheon Books.

Graatrud, Gabrielle. 2016. *SKAM*-frustasjon skapte Viral Hit. *Dagbladet*, May 25.

Grainge, Paul, and Catherine Johnson. 2015. *Promotional Screen Industries*. London and New York: Routledge.

Gray, Jonathan. 2010. *Show Sold Separately. Promos, Spoilers, and Other Media Paratexts*. New York: New York University Press.

Grossberg, Lawrence. 1992. Is There a Fan in the House? The Affective Sensibility of Fandom. In *The Adoring Audience: Fan Culture and Popular Media*, ed. Lisa A. Lewis, 50–65. New York: Routledge.

Gulliksen, Hildri. 2017. Head of NRK Super, in-person interview, Oslo, 19 May.

Guttu, Ane Hjort. 2016. Minutt for Minutt. *Kunstkritikk*, 23 December.

Harrington, C. Lee, and Denis D. Bielby. 1995. *Soap Fans. Pursuing Pleasure and Making Meaning in Everyday Life*. Philadelphia: Temple University Press.

Helle, Birk Tjeldflaat. 2019. Strømmesuksess for 'Parterapi' – sett over en million ganger. *Dagens Næringsliv*, 28 October.

Helsingen, Arne. 2015. Head of Television at NRK, in-person interview, Oslo, 16 January.

Hepp, Andreas, and Nick Couldry. 2010. Introduction: Media Events in Globalized Media Culture. In *Media Events in a Global Age*, eds. Nick Couldry, Andreas Hepp, and Friedrich Krotz, 1–20. London and New York: Routledge.

Hesmondhalgh, David. 2007. *The Cultural Industries*. Los Angeles, London, New Delhi and Singapore: Sage Publications.

Hill, Annette. 2019. *Media Experiences. Engaging with Drama and Reality Television*. London and New York: Routledge.

Hills, Matt. 2002. *Fan Cultures*. London and New York: Routledge.

———. 2015. *Doctor Who: The Unfolding Event*. Basingstoke: Palgrave Macmillan.

———. 2018. Always-on Fandom, Waiting and Bingeing. Psychoanalysis as an Engagement with Fans' 'Infra-Ordinary' Experiences. In *The Routledge Companion to Media Fandom*, eds. Melissa A. Click and S. Suzanne Scott, 18–26. New York and London: Routledge.

Horton, Donald, and R. Richard Wohl. 1956. Mass Communication and Parasocial Interaction: Observations on Intimacy at a Distance. *Psychiatry* 19: 215–229.

Ihlebæk, Karoline A., Trine Syvertsen, and Espen Ytreberg. 2014. Keeping Them and Moving Them: TV Scheduling in the Phase of Channel and Platform Proliferation. *Television and New Media* 15 (5): 470–486.

Jenkins, Henry. 1992. *Textual Poachers. Television Fans & Participatory Culture*. New York: Routledge.

———. 2006. *Convergence Culture. Where Old and New Media Collide*. New York and London: New York University Press.

Jensen, Jolie. 1992. Fandom as Pathology: The Consequences of Characterization. In *The Adoring Audience: Fan Culture and Popular Media*, ed. Lisa A. Lewis, 9–29. New York: Routledge.

Jerslev, Anne. 2017. *SKAM*'s 'lige her' og 'lige nu'. Om *SKAM* og nærvær. *Nordisk Tidsskrift for Informationsvidenskab og kulturformidling* 62 (2): 75–81.

Johnson, Catherine. 2019. *Online TV*. London and New York: Routledge.

King, Anthony. 2001. Violent Pasts: Collective Memory and Football Hooliganism. *The Sociological Review* 49 (4): 568–585.

King-O'Riain, Rebecca Chiyoko. 2020. 'They were Having So Much Fun, So Genuinely…': K-pop Fan Online Affect and Corroborated Authenticity. *New Media & Society*. Online first. https://doi.org/10.1177/1461444820941194.

Kjus, Yngvar. 2009. *Event Media. Television Production Crossing Media Boundaries*. PhD thesis, University of Oslo.

Køhn, Ivar. 2017. Head of NRK Drama, in-person interview, Oslo, 29 November.

Lang-Ree, Kari Anne. 2017. In-house Lawyer at NRK, in-person interview, Oslo, 27 October.

Lilyhammer. Rubicon TV for NRK and Netflix. 2012–2014.

Lindtner, Synnøve Skarsbø, and John Magnus Dahl. 2019. Aligning Adolescent to the Public Sphere: The Teen Serial *Skam* and Democratic Aesthetic. *Javnost—The Public* 26 (1): 54–69.

Lost. ABC. 2004–2010.

Lotz, Amanda D. 2007. *The Television Will Be Revolutionized*. New York: New York University Press.

———., ed. 2009. *Beyond Prime Time. Television Programming in the Post-Network Era*. New York: Routledge.

———. 2017. *Portals: A Treatise on Internet-Distributed Television*. Michigan Publishing.

Magnus, Mari. 2016. *SKAM* – når fiksjon og virkelighet møtes. *Nordicom Information* 38 (2): 31–38.

———. 2017. Online Producer on *SKAM*, in-person interview, Oslo, 12 January.

Melbø, Karine Brøste. 2017. Head of Casting on *blank* at NRK, in-person interview, Oslo, 23 November.

Miége, Bernard. 1989. *The Capitalization of Cultural Production*. New York: International General.

Næsheim, Knut. 2017. Director and Writer (Showrunner) on *blank* at NRK, in-person interview, Oslo, 27 September.

Nordlie, Hege Gaarder. 2017. Assistant Scriptwriter on *blank* at NRK, in-person interview, Oslo, 6 December.

NRK. 2013. *NRKs årsrapport 2013*. Oslo: NRK.

NTB. 2017. 'Skam'-skole Stenger Dørene for Danske Fans. *Aftenposten*, 9 January.

Nyborg, Ingvill Marie. 2012. *MIA* – et stort og stille drama på nett. *NRKBeta. no*, 3 May.

Øverlie, Tom. 2017. Online Developer on *SKAM* and *blank* at NRK P3 Event and Development, in-person interview, Oslo, 5 December.

Pearson, Roberta. 2010. Fandom in the Digital Era. *Popular Communication*, 8 (1): 84–95.

Pedersen, Bernt Erik. 2019. Ikke siden 'Skam' har NRK-seerne strømmet en dramaserie like mye som den denne. *Dagsavisen*, 22 October.

Petersen, Line Nybro, and Vilde Schanke Sundet. 2019. Play Moods across the Life Course in *SKAM* Fandom. *Journal of Fandom Studies* 7 (2): 113–131.

Revheim, Hanna Huglen, and Pedja Kalajdzic. 2017. Dansker på 'Skam'-safari: -Vi synes det er så gøy. *NRK*, 11 April.

Sandvoss, Cornel. 2005. *Fans: The Mirror of Consumption*. Cambridge: Polity Press.

Scannell, Paddy. 2014. *Television and the Meaning of Life: An Enquiry into the Human Situation*. Cambridge: Polity Press.

SKAM/SHAME. NRK. 2015–2017.

Skarstein, Dag. 2018. Lesingar av *Skam* – seriens kommentarfelt som tolknings-felleskap. In *Dramaserien Skam. Analytike perspektiver og didaktiske muligheter*, eds. Synnøve Skarsbø Lindtner and Dag Skarstein, 197–219. Bergen: Fagbokforlaget.

Sørensen, Håkon Lund. 2017a. *SKAM* Statistic. Internal Document Given by E-mail, 17 February.

———. 2017b. *SKAM* Statistic. Internal Document Given by E-mail, 20 September.

———. 2019. SKAM Statistic. Internal Document Given by E-mail, 7 May.

Sprus, Nathalie. 2018. NRK's Press Contact on *SKAM* and *blank* at NRK, in-person interview, Oslo, 19 February.

Sundet, Vilde Schanke. 2017. 'Det er bare du som kan føle det du føler' – emosjonell inverstering og engasjement i nettdramaet *SKAM*. *16:9 film-tidsskrift*, 25 June.

———. 2019. From Secret Online Teen Drama to International Cult Phenomenon: The Global Expansion of SKAM and its Public Service Mission. *Critical Studies in Television* 15(1): 69-90.

Sundet, Vilde Schanke, and Espen Ytreberg. 2009. Working Notions of Active Audiences: Further Research on the Active Participant in Convergent Media Industries. *Convergence* 15 (4): 383–390.

Sundet, Vilde Schanke, and Line Nybro Petersen. 2020. Ins and Outs of Transmedia Fandom: Motives for Entering and Exiting the *SKAM* Fan Community Online. *Poetics*. Online first. https://doi.org/10.1016/j.poetic.2020.101510.

Svendsen, Maiken. 2016. Derfor skjermer NRK 'Skam'-skuespillerne. *VG*, 16 February.

Teen Wolf. MTV, 2011–2017. MTV.

The Matrix. 1999. Warner Bros.

The Vampire Diaries. 2009–2017. CW.

Todd, Anne Marie. 2011. Saying Goodbye to Friends: Fan Culture as Lived Experience. *Journal of Popular Culture* 44 (4): 854–871.

Tolonen, Kristian. 2015. Lilyhammer Statistic. An Internal Document Given by E-mail, 6 February.

Van den Bulck, Hilde, and Hallvard Moe. 2017. Public Service Media, Universality and Personalization through Algorithms: Mapping Strategies and Exploring Dilemmas. *Media, Culture & Society* 40 (6): 875–892.

Villumsen, Katrine Villareal. 2016. Utsolgt på 10 minutter: 350 danske fans spiste fiskekaker og tok farvel med *Skam*. *Aftenposten*, 19 December.

Wallace, Petter. 2015. Head of External Productions at NRK, in-person interview, Oslo, 15 January.

Williams, Raymond. 2005 [1974]. *Television: Technology and Cultural Form*. London: Routledge.

Williams, Rebecca. 2015. *Post-Object Fandom. Television, Identify and Self-Narrative*. New York: Bloomsbury.

———. 2017. Fan Tourism and Pilgrimage. In *The Routledge Companion to Media Fandom*, eds. Melissa A. Click and Suzanne Scott. New York: Routledge.

Woldsdal, Nicolay, and Ingunn Michelsen. 2016. *Skam* slår alle rekorder. *NRK.no*, 21 December.

Ytreberg, Espen. 2009. Extended Liveness and Eventfulness in Multi-platform Reality Formats. *New Media & Society* 11 (4): 467–485.

———. forthcoming. *Media and Events in History*. Book under contract, forthcoming at Polity Press.

CHAPTER 5

Changing Industry–Audience Relations

Abstract This chapter discusses how streaming affects *industry–audience relations*—that is, how the industry perceives its audience and tries to attract them, measure them, and build loyal and engaging relationships with them. It revisits the concept of 'audience making' and looks at new opportunities for accommodating the audience in the move from linear to on-demand consumption models, as well as the value of measuring audience engagement and fan activity when gauging a show's success. It is organised according to the three ways streaming impacts industry–audience relations: the way the industry *perceives its audience*, the way the industry *serves particularly interested audiences (i.e. fans)* and the way the industry uses the audiences to *measure success*. As elsewhere in the narrative, this chapter relies upon *Lilyhammer*, *SKAM* and *blank* to illustrate the key tendencies and arguments.

Keywords Audience making • Audience relations • Audiences • Fans • Industry • Streaming • Television drama

V. S. Sundet, *Television Drama in the Age of Streaming*, https://doi.org/10.1007/978-3-030-66418-3_5

Introduction

How does streaming affect *industry–audience relations*—that is, the relationship between the television industry and its audience? Drawing upon the earlier discussions of industry perceptions of streaming (Chap. 2), new production cultures (Chap. 3) and changing publishing strategies (Chap. 4), the present chapter addresses the specific ways in which streaming and digital media allow for new and more direct relations between the industry and its audiences and fans. It builds on the understanding that this relation is formed by 'push-pull dynamics' (Hill 2019), in that the push-and-pull between producers and audiences works both ways and is related to power (see also Jensen and Jacobsen 2020).

A key argument of this chapter is that streaming impacts industry–audience relations in at least three ways. First, it affects how the industry *perceives its audience* and tries to attract them, measure them, and build loyal and engaging relationships with them. By revisiting the concept of 'audience making' (Ang 2005 [1991]; Ettema and Whitney 1994b), this chapter looks at how the audience is accommodated in new ways when television is consumed online and on-demand, and how audience engagement and loyalty become critical means of assessing success. As such, this chapter investigates the complex and sometimes contradictory set of audience categories that drama producers are increasingly bound to serve, including national and international, linear and on-demand, and mass and niche audiences. *Lilyhammer*, *SKAM* and *blank* are all useful examples of this relation, as they were produced to accommodate different audience groups in various markets using many publishing platforms. Second, this chapter addresses how streaming invites the industry to prioritise *particularly invested audience groups—that is, fans*—as a means of building loyalty, engagement and activities surrounding television shows. This chapter argues that streaming and digital media make it easier for the audience to become fans and engage in fan communities online, but also that streaming and digital media make fans and fan communities more attractive to the television industry, and it discusses the outcome of this dual interest in 'the fan'. *Lilyhammer*, *SKAM* and *blank* are productive examples here as well, as they each created large international fan bases (Bore 2017; Petersen and Sundet 2019; Sundet and Petersen 2020). Third, this chapter addresses how streaming affects the way the industry *measures success* in a changing television market. The main argument here is that the new industry–audience relations arranged by streaming contest established success measures within the industry and demonstrate the need for new measures. As such, this chapter confronts the shift from the analogue world of television, where eyeballs watching a screen defined both the audience and the show's (and the broadcaster's) success, to a digital on-demand world, where linear audience ratings are called into question (Bourdon and Méadel 2014b). As a result, conventional practices—and even the industry's fundamental business model—are starting to show their age (Johnson 2019; Lotz 2018).[1]

THE PARADOX OF AUDIENCE MAKING

The first impact of streaming on industry–audience relations concerns the ways in which the industry perceives its audience, often labelled 'audience making' in the literature (Ang 2005 [1991]). This term evokes the broader concept of the 'imagined audience' often used by social media scholars as a 'mental conceptualization of the people with whom we are communicating' (Litt 2012: 331)—the imagined audience, that is, serves as a 'guide for what is appropriate and relevant to share when an actual audience is unknown or not physically present' (Litt and Hargittai 2016: 1). This notion highlights the fact that the less available an actual audience is, the more dependent stakeholders become on their imaginations to make up for the absence (Marwick and boyd 2010); furthermore, the imagined audience can be just as influential as the actual audience in determining industry behaviour (Baldwin and Holmes 1987).

The term 'audience making', relatedly, refers to how 'communicators make audiences' (Ettema and Whitney 1994a: 4)—that is, how media workers make sense of the audience, attract it, measure it and try to serve it. The term has its roots in Raymond Williams's (1961) early work on television but reaches its apex in the 1990s through the work of Ien Ang (2005 [1991]) and others (Ettema and Whitney 1994b). At that time, as seen within a commercial US television landscape, 'the audience' was

---

[1] Part of this chapter builds on an interview study with fifty Scandinavian *SKAM* fans between thirteen and seventy years of age which was conducted in collaboration with Line Nybro Petersen (see Chap. 1). This study is also addressed in earlier publications, most importantly Petersen and Sundet 2019 (*Play moods across the life course in SKAM fandom*) and Sundet and Petersen 2020 (*Ins and outs of fandom: Motives for entering and exiting the SKAM fan community online*). The argument that 'audience making' still holds value in a streaming television market is also presented in Sundet 2016 (*Still 'desperately seeking the audience'? Audience making in the age of media convergence (the Lilyhammer experience)*).

often described as an aggregated mass—a commodity—to be sold to advertisers, and Ang found a television industry devoted to 'conquering, measuring and serving' its audience in order to thrive. According to Ang, however, the audience was 'extremely difficult to define, attract and keep' (2005 [1991]: ix), and, she argued, there was a disparity between the real audience—that is, actual individuals watching television with their own needs and interests—and 'the audience' as a creation of the industry that served or justified *its* needs and interests. Drawing on the ideas of Michel Foucault, Ang stressed that knowledge was one of the defining components of power and that defining the audience was actually about controlling it. A fundamental task in television production became, therefore, to 'make an audience' (see also Bourdon and Méadel 2014a). A public service broadcaster (like NRK) works with notions of its audience which are different from those of the private and commercial television players, although audience making remains very important. For instance, Trine Syvertsen (2004) has shown how the NRK originally defined 'the audience' in terms of citizens and saw its role as serving the public interest—that is, giving them what they need in addition to what they want. Gradually, however, NRK incorporated other audience notions as well—including notions of the audience as active participants and players.

The term 'audience making' still holds value for the analysis of industry–audience relations today, for at least three reasons (Sundet 2016). To start with, the term points to the fact that 'the audience' is always constructed; it simply does not exist in any natural grouping. As mentioned, Ang (2005 [1991]) highlighted the disparity between the 'real audience' and 'the audience', echoing Williams's observation that there are no actual 'masses', 'only ways of seeing people as masses' (2005 [1974]: 289). Second, the term points to the fact that industry notions of 'the audience' influence media production. To illustrate, whether the industry views its audience as active or passive, nomadic or roaming, experimental or goal-oriented, or national or international influences how it plans for its productions (see also Chap. 2). Third, the term points to the fact that strategic interests influence industry notions. As Ang points out, 'the audience' has to be conceived of as 'addressable, attainable, winnable, in short, a manoeuvrable "thing"' (2005 [1991]: 23; see also Napoli 2003). Thus, the way the media *wants* to see its audience influences the way it *does* see it (see also Sundet and Ytreberg 2009).

Early literature highlights two key problems when the industry is 'making an audience'—first, that the industry does not have enough data on audiences and their habits and preferences, and, second, that this data, when available, is unable to inform complex notions of the audience. Streaming resolves some of these challenges but creates new ones as well—a situation I call the *paradox of audience making*: in the age of streaming, the amount of information about the audience is almost inexhaustible, but the challenge to the industry of making sense of it all is profound. Whereas audiences before mainly meant eyeballs measured via ratings and market shares—that is, information that reduced them to an aggregated (yet manageable) mass (Ang 2005 [1991])—audiences today leave behind many traces for the industry to analyse and unpack. These traces include not only traditional ratings and market shares but also big data from streaming services, qualitative and quantitative data from various social media platforms and paratexts, and insight and feedback gained through the extensive use of audience interviews, workshops and screenings. In all, today's traces tell us not only how many viewers there are but also, potentially, who they are, where they are, how they navigate and how much affection (or disaffection) they display in their consumption. A lot of data, of course, does not automatically imply productive data *analysis*, and the analysis itself demands time, tools and knowledge. For the television industry, then, audience making begs several questions: How much data should be collected about the audience, how should the industry make sense of it and how should data-driven insights inform the production and publishing of television?

As illustrated in Chap. 2, retaining—and, along the way, getting to know—the audience is described as crucial to NRK. As one executive put it, 'If there is one word I use several times a day, it is "the audience, the audience, the audience". We are very dependent on understanding them to make sure they are given value for their money' (Wallace interviewed 2015). Although digitisation, streaming and globalisation have all impacted industry–audience relations, nothing indicates that knowledge of 'the audience' has become *less* important to industry executives. On the contrary, it was always top of mind for the informants, many of whom described how audience insight was being prioritised across more and more of NRK's organisation (Haugen interviewed 2015; Lund interviewed 2015; Tolonen interviewed 2015).

Furthermore, new development tools such as the NABC model and the design-thinking approach are increasingly used to incorporate an audience perspective into programme production (Haugen interviewed 2015; Hedemann interviewed 2017; see also Chap. 3). For instance, during the ten-year analysis period (2010–2019), the NABC model informed a range of different NRK productions, from news and entertainment to event shows and drama (Hedemann 2014). It is best known as the development tool driving NRK Super's online drama successes (*Sara*, *MIA* and *Jenter/ Girls*), which later guided both *SKAM* and *blank*'s massive appropriation of audience insights, in addition to that of many other NRK youth series (Johansson 2020). All these series used audience insights to identify not only audience needs but also ways to reflect the audience in a relevant and realistic manner (see also Sundet 2019). One informant explained that the very idea of making online drama in the first place grew out of an audience interview NRK did—following the NABC model—with a young Norwegian girl in 2007, where she expressed her desire for 'an online best friend who lives and resembles her, who is in the same situation as her, but who lives a more exciting life' (Gulliksen interviewed 2017; see also Faldalen 2016).

The NABC model is not only a crucial means of identifying audience needs at the beginning of a production but also a 'way of thinking' throughout the whole process, *blank*'s Showrunner notes: 'The NABC model is not something you do once, and then you are done with it, it is something you do to a greater or lesser extent in *every* choice you make. (…) We try to think like the target audience group at every stage, in every choice' (Næsheim interviewed 2017). Making an audience, then, is a continuous process. Likewise, several *blank* informants emphasised how they used the massive casting process—including more than 1900 youths for the first season alone—to understand the target audience (Melbø interviewed 2017; Selim interviewed 2017), how they spent time online to understand the target audience's social media habits (Aspeflaten interviewed 2017; Nordlie interviewed 2017) and how they monitored audience responses across various platforms during each season as part of the game (Fossbakken interviewed 2018; Næsheim interviewed 2018). Several informants also described how each season brought a new 'dialogue' with the audience which allowed them to extend their familiarity with it (Akrim interviewed 2018; Erlandsen interviewed 2017; Øverlie interviewed 2017; see also Chap. 3). Clearly, for some of them, audience making means entering a mediated relationship. Such a connection is possible precisely because these online drama shows serve small, niche audiences instead of 'the nation'—distinct audience groups give the opportunity to go close.

Nevertheless, this expanded focus on audience needs, insights and data is, as described in Chap. 3, challenging for various reasons. To start with, it is very time consuming to keep up with the audience, not least in series like *SKAM* and *blank*, which spread across many platforms with massive audience response and fan activities. As already described, *SKAM*'s four seasons generated close to 140,000 approved comments on the blog (skam.p3.no) alone (Erlandsen 2018), which meant that merely catching up with the debate on the blog took time away from other aspects of the production. Besides, not everyone was fond of getting direct feedback every day, and some found their professional instincts inappropriately contested or disturbed (Nordlie interviewed 2018). Furthermore, the rush to identify audience needs and serve niche segments can also mean misreading audience demands or giving specific aspects too much weight. For example, in the case of *blank*, there was an ongoing tension between serving the audience's perceived needs without allowing the show to appear too realistic and therefore slow or even tedious (Næsheim interview 2018).

Audience making is also put to the test when a show's actual audience grows beyond its intended audience—an eventuality which the global television market increasingly enables (see also Chap. 3). For example, *Lilyhammer*, *SKAM* and *blank* all attracted a much broader international audience base than what was anticipated. *Lilyhammer* was exported internationally through Netflix and the distribution company Red Arrow, redefining the intended national public service audience to also include an international (US) streaming audience (Sundet 2016; see also Bore 2017). *SKAM* and *blank* were exported internationally by the national audience itself, as fans took it upon themselves to share and translate content into various languages for one another. In addition to gaining a large international contingent, *SKAM* and *blank* also expanded their target niche audience from teens and youths to practically all age groups (Petersen and Sundet 2019).

Many informants expressed ambivalence when evaluating the consequences of serving both national and global audiences, and, with regard to *SKAM* and *blank*, both younger and older audiences as well. On the one hand, they applauded the widespread sharing of these stories so that more people could enjoy them and learn from them. One *SKAM* informant said, referring to Isak's storyline in season 3, 'If we can tell a story of importance for a gay Filipino boy, it is wonderful' (Magnus interviewed 2017). Another executive added, 'It is great fun that fans have taken *SKAM* out into the world, and it fits perfectly with our promotion strategy. (…) It's wonderful that so many fans internationally embrace the show' (Furevold-Boland interviewed 2016). Likewise, *Lilyhammer* informants emphasised the importance of making good stories regardless of their intended geographical markets or audience segments. Many also highlighted the fact that international and local audiences did not necessarily conflict, as stories which 'everyone could relate to' could always be told with a 'local twist or frame' (Kolbjørnsen interviewed 2015; see also Sundet 2016; Waade et al. 2020).

On the other hand, a large international audience (and fan base) clearly put these shows to the test, and a key challenge for each of them was to keep the focus on the Norwegian audience even when international audiences vastly outnumbered this intended segment. One *SKAM* informant explained, '*SKAM*'s contribution to an international audience is fantastic, but it is not our job to tell stories internationally. We tell stories from a Norwegian perspective, and we will continue to do so' (Magnus interviewed 2017). Other informants pointed to NRK as a public service broadcaster with a mission of serving Norwegian (not international) audiences: 'Our business is to create content for Norwegians. (…) Our license money will go to our license payers' (Lang-Ree interviewed 2017).

Informants from both *SKAM* and *blank* also expressed concerns about becoming too popular with older age groups and thus losing credibility and traction with the younger target group. In fact, in both productions, a lot of work was done to try to *avoid* the allegiance of older viewers. For example, both series developed distinctly youthful promotion and publishing strategies, using music, slang and pop-cultural references to signal teen and youth ownership of the content. Neither series was reluctant to use cultural codes which older audiences would find foreign or exclusive. This intense focus on younger audience groups is also evident in *SKAM* and *blank*'s high prioritisation of the mobile phone as a device for content consumption, as these production teams knew that this device was essential to reaching young viewers (Akrim interviewed 2017; Erlandsen interviewed 2017; Øverlie interviewed 2017).

Both series, however, eventually saw a flood of feedback from a fan base which, in Scandinavia at least, leaned towards women in the age group of thirty to fifty years old (Petersen and Sundet 2019; see also Lindtner and Dahl 2020). The heavy participation from older audiences was an issue for both productions, but it felt particularly threatening to informants on the smaller show *blank*, who feared that the older audiences would push aside young viewers and make the show come off as 'old' and generally 'uncool'

(Aspeflaten interviewed 2017; Næsheim interviewed 2017). *SKAM*'s overwhelming success, on the other hand, meant that over the course of its four seasons, it had to 'give up' on its 'teen-only' strategy and accept its identity as a much broader cultural phenomenon (Erlandsen interviewed 2017).

Serving Fans and Fan Cultures

The second aspect of changing industry–audience relations involves how the industry aims to serve a particularly invested audience group, its fans, in order to increase loyalty, engagement and activity. Crucial to this aspect is the fact that streaming and digital media make it easier for audiences to become fans and take part in fan activities. At the same time, streaming and digital media also make it more attractive for the *industry* to serve audiences as fans. Hence, we see a push–pull tendency in which both audience and industry interests come together in digital fan servicing.

Responding to the audience as active participants and fans is not a new phenomenon within the television industry, and it has been analysed and theorised in fan studies for decades (Baym 2000; Evans 2011; Harrington and Bielby 1995; Hills 2002; Jenkins 2006). However, digital technology and social media have made it easier for fans to take part in fan activities and find other fans with similar interests online. Henry Jenkins uses the term 'participatory culture' to describe the dynamic through which 'fans and other consumers are invited to actively participate in the creation and circulation of new content' (2006: 290). Similarly, Roberta Pearson demonstrates the profound impact of the 'digital revolution' on fans and fandom, 'empowering and disempowering, blurring the lines between producers and consumers, creating symbiotic relationships between powerful corporations and individual fans, and giving rise to new forms of cultural production' (2010: 84). Underlying these observations is the awareness that fan audiences were long 'ridiculed' by television executives (Gray et al. 2007: 4) and associated with negative, often pathological stereotypes of fans as obsessed, deviant, hysterical and fanatic (Jensen 1992: 9; see also Jenkins 1992: chapter 1). Fans, that is, have not always been welcomed—or even sought after—by the industry and especially not by public service institutions such as NRK, which was devoted instead to serving its audience as citizens (Syvertsen 2004).

Today, the media industry has developed a more nuanced take on both fans and fan cultures. Furthermore, several studies have addressed how fan service furthers the strategic interests of the media (Evans 2020; Hill 2019; Jenkins 2006). To begin with, serving viewers as fans means serving loyal audiences who will not only watch every episode but also purchase ancillary products. According to Pearson (2010), this insight motivated many 1990s television producers to design shows specifically for cult niches, among them *Twin Peaks* (ABC, 1990–1991) and *X-Files* (FOX, 1993–2002) (see also Hills 2002). In the age of streaming, a loyal audience is even more critical, as loyalty pulls people back to specific programmes again and again (see also Chap. 2). Second, attracting loyal audiences and fans is a means of spreading positive content to others—publicity and buzz, that is, derive from a tighter industry–audience relation (Gray 2010). As argued by one informant with experience from both *SKAM* and *blank*, 'if they love you, they will do the promotion job for you' (Øverlie interviewed 2017). Third, loyal audiences and fans also extend transmedia story worlds and help to make fictional universes more immersive and engaging (Evans 2020; Hills 2002; see also Chap. 4). As shown in the previous two chapters, fans served all of these functions for *Lilyhammer*, *SKAM* and *blank* (see also Bore 2017; Sundet 2019; Sundet and Petersen 2020).

Figure 5.1 gives an example of fan drawing of the couple from season 3 of *SKAM*, Isak and Even, made by Miriam Latu and posted on her

Fig. 5.1   Fan drawing of Isak and Even, couple from season 3 of *SKAM*

Instagram account (@om_hundre_ar_er_allting) November 15, 2017. Used with permission.

Serving the audience as fans also means entering into a deeper relationship with them. Annette Hill uses the term 'spectrum of engagement' to describe the cognitive and affective work of producers and audiences—work which 'extends across an emotional range when people switch between positive and negative engagement, or disengagement' (2019: 54–55; see also Hill and Steemers 2017). Similarly, many fan scholars show how the fan's engagement and connectedness with their fan object can strengthen and deepen their television experiences (Baym 2000; Hills 2002; Jenkins 1992; Sandvoss 2005). For instance, C. Lee Harrington and Denise D. Bielby (1995) find in their study of soap opera fans that sharing fandom is often seen as an indicator of compatibility, thus transforming fandom into an arena of intimacy (1995: 87; see also Cavicchi 1998). Scholars have also demonstrated how fans can have a lifelong relationship with their fan object (Kuhn 2012) and how television fandoms endure after the show has ended (Williams 2015).

Interviews with *SKAM* fans touch upon all the aforementioned aspects (see also Sundet and Petersen 2020). For example, several *SKAM* fans describe an immediate, almost explosive fascination with the show which practically forced them to connect with others who might feel the same. As they entered into fan communities, as well, many found the experience surprisingly enjoyable, and almost all of the informants reported making new friends through the *SKAM* fandom and even meeting up in real life. Many also described the ways in which partaking in fan communities—and discussing every detail in every clip—made them love the show even more. These sentiments echo findings from fan studies correlating time invested and degree of affection (Whetmore and Kielwasser 1983: 11) and showing how meaning production is often a social and public process (Jenkins 1992: 75).

Serving the audience as fans does not imply that the interests of the industry and the audience are always aligned or that the industry has given away its power and control to the audience. It is instead often the opposite, and fan studies are full of stories about the tensions, confrontations and conflicts between the television industry and its fans (Jenkins 1992, 2006; see also Gray 2003). Several studies also show how some fans are prioritised over others by the industry. Kristina Busse (2007) observes, 'Certain groups of fans became legit if and only if they follow certain ideas, don't become too rebellious, too pornographic, don't read the text too much against the grain'. Thus, tension persists even though both the audiences themselves and the industry see the value of fandoms.

In the rest of this section, I will turn my attention to the challenges involved in the ways in which *blank* worked to serve its young intended audience as fans. The show operated with this as an explicit and outspoken goal (Hole interviewed 2017; Næsheim interviewed 2017), and discussions about how to do this best recurred in both internal meetings and interviews. The motivation for serving the audience as fans was embedded in the online drama format: It built on the idea that audiences should not only watch but also *discuss* these series to learn from the moral dilemmas they presented. In short, the idea was that the target audience would become better prepared to master difficulties in their own lives by 'working through' (Ellis 2000) realistic scenarios by debating these issues with others. The *blank* production team, then, actively deployed audience engagement and cultivated emotional investment in order to generate debates (Lindtner and Dahl 2019; Sundet 2017). As explained by one informant, who also wrote and directed season 1, 'One significant advantages of real-time online drama is that you publish the story without telling when the next update is coming. You create space where key drama questions can linger. The audience wonder what happens next and they discuss with each other' (Næsheim interviewed 2017). Relatedly, *SKAM*'s Online Producer explained, 'When the dramaturgy gets intense, and you do not really care if Isak is a fictional character or a friend you follow online—that is when you get unique engagement. That is when you have to follow and have to discuss it' (Magnus interviewed 2017).

The interest in serving an active and participatory audience which spends time discussing the show is also evident in the informants' concern about distractions such as other real-time online drama series. For example, several informants worried that *blank* was being released at the same time as other real-time online dramas (including *Lovleg* and several *SKAM* remakes) and speculated about how many shows the audience could take part in at the same time, thanks to the intense and tight relationships they encouraged: 'Real-time online drama is about making people want more, and if you close all the gaps with other real-time dramas, I am afraid it can be too tiring for people. I am afraid people will not manage to keep up' (Nordlie interviewed 2017).

Among the strategies *blank* used to address its target audience as active participants and fans was its publishing model of spreading content across platforms in real-time (see also Chap. 4). The comments section it included following every update, as well, signalled that the show expected the audience to take part. However, the *blank* team also used more indirect strategies in relation to the intended audience group. For example, the team worked hard to create 'ambassadors' among youths from all over the country (Selim interviewed 2017) to help recruit people to the casting process. The production also used ambassadors to promote the show, which, in the first season, followed the *SKAM* strategy of avoiding official promotion and press packages and instead capitalising on the power of word-of-mouth (see also Sundet 2019). According to one informant, 'We tried to avoid big news stories. We talked about the fear of Dagbladet [tabloid newspaper] heading the story "new *SKAM* is casting now"' (Selim interviewed 2017). Instead of using standard approaches or even the existing *SKAM* fan network, *blank* promoted its first season exclusively by sending messages to its 'ambassadors' and cast members, hoping to signal to everyone that *blank* aimed for a close relationship with the target audience.

As mentioned above, tension persisted nevertheless. To start with, there was ongoing tension within the production team regarding how many fan activities the production should enable. While some members of the team wanted to explore a range of activities—involving Easter eggs, intertextual references, clues and codes—others were more protective of the storyline and convinced that these fan initiatives would disturb the story and serve some members of the audience (the fans) at the expense of others (the target youth audience in general). Another critical challenge regarding fan service was that it took attention away from the target audience. In fact, many of the most active *blank* fans were the thirty- or forty-year-old women who crossed over from *SKAM* to *blank*. They were both active and productive but did not fall within *blank*'s (or *SKAM*'s) target age group. A dilemma which followed *blank* through all three seasons was therefore how to continue to invite the younger audiences as participants without alienating the most productive fans, many of whom were both international and older than the show's target audience (Hole interviewed 2018; Næsheim interviewed 2018).

A lesson from *blank* which resonates with *SKAM* as well is that a show can address its audience as active participants and fans and even attract a huge fan base, but it may not reflect your intended niche or transform the show into a media-generated event (as described in the previous chapter). Here again are the complex push–pull dynamics of the contemporary television industry: the project teams can extend the invitation, but they cannot guarantee that the intended audience will show up.

How to Measure Success?

The third aspect of how streaming affects industry–audience relations involves how the industry measures success. 'Success', of course, is a flexible and relative term which is used in different ways by different industry players. In the previous chapters, I have given many examples of how industry executives evaluate the success of content and programmes, sometimes even operating with different definitions of success for the very same programme. For instance, Rubicon TV, NRK and Netflix all defined *Lilyhammer* as a success but for very different reasons (see Chap. 3; see also Sundet 2016). Several *blank* informants noted that being the descendant of *SKAM* was particularly challenging, because *SKAM* 'achieved success on every conceivable parameter' (Erlandsen interviewed 2017): it broke viewing records on linear and on-demand channels; generated massive traffic on its website (skam.p3.no); received critical acclaim through reviews, prizes and nominations; was exported internationally by fans and remakes; generated publicity, buzz and debates in the public sphere; and, perhaps most importantly, had a deep and, for some, life-changing impact on peoples' lives.

Nevertheless, one persistent parameter of success both over time and across different national television markets is audience measurement—the total number of viewers or market share (Bourdon and Méadel 2014b; Napoli 2011). In Norway, official audience measurement was introduced with the commercial television channels in the early 1990s, but it soon became an important tool for NRK as well (Syvertsen 1997). A key reason why audience measurement is so relied upon in the television industry is that it serves as an official currency of sorts (Napoli 2003; see also Lotz 2007). Industry players use audience numbers when selling advertising slots, positioning themselves in relation to one another, and distributing budgets, personnel and resources internally. Bigger audiences often lead to bigger budgets as well as more prestige. As such, audience measurement is an essential part of 'making an audience' (Ang 2005 [1991]), as discussed above. Streaming, however, increases the complexity of the industry—through its new players, forms of distribution and publishing strategies—and therefore contests both established industry–audience relations and measurement techniques in several ways.

To start with, streaming and on-demand television allow viewers to watch when they want and where they want, meaning that audience measurement must account for various distribution techniques (linear, on-demand and web) and devices (television, personal computer, mobile phone or tablet) (see also Chap. 4). The duality of consumption of both linear and non-linear television—depending on the content, context and mood—likewise forces these measurements to incorporate both 'new' and 'old' viewer habits (see also Bruun 2020). In Norway, the company responsible for official television measurement (Kantar) readily changed its methods to include both viewing modes, and all the critical national television players settled upon the new measurement as the official 'currency'. It could not, however, incorporate the global streaming services— among them Netflix, HBO and Disney Plus—because they are not transparent about viewing figures. The reasons for this are probably many. If the service does not share its numbers, it controls the narrative around a programme's success or failure. Furthermore, streaming services often operate with differing definitions of 'a view'. For a streaming service, as well, measurements other than viewing numbers are important too—for instance, a programme's ability to generate buzz, attract new subscribers or keep viewers watching for a longer period. For national television players—rooted in broadcasting and embracing the tradition of a shared currency—the lack of transparency is, however, troublesome, as it provides little information about one's competitors. In the case of *Lilyhammer*, for instance, NRK would share their viewing numbers on NRK's platforms (linear and on-demand) but knew little about how the show performed on Netflix in international markets or how audiences behaved while watching the show on Netflix.

Second, streaming and on-demand television allow for time-shifted viewing and binge-watching, meaning that the time of measurement can be hard to define and agree on. For instance, how long after a television programme is published should the ratings be reported—that is, how long should a programme have to gather views? While television programmes in a scheduled and linear context typically deliver viewing numbers the next day, programmes in a streaming context sometimes need more time to add up their views, as many viewers like to wait for a whole season to binge all at once. Hence, several informants complained that the 'old' measurement techniques of defining a show's success one day later would fail to cover success stories in a streaming landscape, where some programmes needed time 'to grow' (Sørensen interviewed 2017). Relatedly, some viewers watch the same programmes more than once, meaning that viewing numbers will grow over time. For instance, several *SKAM* fans reported having seen the show 'a thousand times' (Woman 21, interviewed 2017) and regularly going back to binge the four seasons again (see also Sørensen 2019).

To complicate the picture even more, some programmes, including real-time online drama, operate with the explicit goal of generating *simultaneous* viewing. For these shows, a critical success parameter is the number of views or visitors any given clip or update would attract *when published* (see also Chap. 4). To illustrate, both *SKAM* and *blank* used Google Analytics daily when new clips were published to track audience behaviour on these shows' websites (skam.p3.no and blank.p3.no). As explained by one informant with experience from both *SKAM* and *blank*:

> The most essential tool for us is the tool that everyone understands. Google Analytics is such a tool—it is easy to use and measure traffic and engagement. In season 1 of *SKAM*, we could use it to see when teens came home from school. Before the '30+ people' discovered *SKAM* and 'ruined' our statistic, we could read the daily life of Norwegian 16-year-olds based on Google Analytics statistics. (Kim Erlandsen, online developer on *SKAM* and *blank*, interviewed 2017)

Third, streaming and on-demand television contest the accuracy of national audience measurement more fundamentally still, as many viewers watch television programmes on several channels and platforms which are not even covered by these methods. One example is *Lilyhammer*, as described above, which lacks its total number of viewers because Netflix withholds information on how the show performed. Both *SKAM* and *blank* generated large audiences which were reflected in official television measurements (*SKAM* in particular), but both also generated large audiences abroad *not* covered in these measurements. For example, *SKAM* and *blank* attracted international audiences who watched fan-translated versions of clips distributed through Dailymotion, Google Drive links or social media sites such as YouTube or Twitter. While piracy viewing is far from new, it stresses the weakness of official audience measurements, especially for television shows generating large, international fan bases. In the case of *SKAM*, the official national audience measurement completely missed the actual numbers of viewers globally.

Finally, many informants noted that streaming and on-demand television put pressure on the industry to incorporate new success criteria altogether. While audience measurements are highly valued by the industry, they fail to incorporate other essential success criteria, such as audience engagement and social impact. For NRK, as a public service broadcaster, these success criteria were particularly significant (see also Chap. 2). For example, many informants highlighted the importance of 'double storytelling' and making television drama with a societal 'footprint', reflecting the overall NRK interest in popular enlightenment (Furevold-Boland interviewed 2017; Køhn interviewed 2017; Rønning interviewed 2015). In short, high audience numbers were important, but they were not enough, and for some shows, they were not even particularly relevant. *SKAM* and *blank*'s main goal, after all, was to reach a target niche audience of teens and youths and engage them, and both shows applied strategies to *avoid* larger audience groups. Thus, high audience numbers might still occur (as *SKAM* certainly indicates), but they were not to be expected as such, as one informant with experience from both *SKAM* and *blank* explained:

> On the one side, I am interested in getting high viewing numbers, but on the other, I keep forgetting what high numbers are [laughter]. It is safe to say that I am concerned about the numbers, but it is less important. I am far more concerned about us making good and important content. (Tore Fossbakken, Post Producer on *blank* and *SKAM*, interviewed 2018)

Relatedly, many informants highlighted the fact that success formulas today are no guarantee of success formulas tomorrow. One said, 'We can never expect our shows to be sold to Netflix. There is one *Lilyhammer* and one *SKAM*. We cannot expect the same to happen again. *SKAM* is probably NRK's biggest success of all time' (Lange-Ree interviewed 2017).

In sum, streaming and on-demand at once challenge established success criteria and invite new ones. The consequence is both a more chaotic debate concerning how to define success criteria and more tailor-made strategies and success measures adapted to different programmes and their specific audiences and goals.

Summing Up

This chapter has analysed how streaming affects industry–audience relations—that is, the ways in which the industry perceives its audience and tries to attract them, measure them, and build loyal and engaging relationships with them. It has explored how the industry perceives its audience, how it serves particularly interested audiences (i.e. fans) and how it uses the audience's behaviours to measure success. All three of these resonate with the challenge of retaining the audience and gaining visibility, as discussed in Chap. 2, and connect with the discussion about changing production cultures and publishing models in Chaps. 3 and 4.

A key argument of this chapter is that streaming introduces a paradox for audience making, in that the amount of information about the audience is now almost inexhaustible but the work of understanding and using it all remains as challenging as ever. The paradox of audience making thus emerges from the massive amount of available data which the audiences leave behind it in the media today, including both official and unofficial channels and platforms. It also points to the fact that many industry executives need to operate with complex notions of the audience—national and international, linear and on-demand, niche and mass.

A second key argument is that serving the audience as followers and fans has become more common in the television industry and that this tendency satisfies both industry and audience interests. As this chapter demonstrates, though, fan service is not without tension, and it can be challenging for the executives involved. It can also take attention away from other tasks and audience groups. Because fans are so active, productive and visible, they risk overshadowing less visible audience groups, which are sometimes more relevant to a particular programme. This is an important insight, as the lessons learned from *SKAM* pushed several youth-oriented productions to serve their audiences as fans, even though young people sometimes avoid such productions because of the intense fan activities (Sundet and Petersen 2020).

This point also ties into the last argument—namely, that streaming contests established success measures in the television industry and suggests new ones. While audience numbers still work as the 'official currency' of the industry, other measurements are starting to take hold, including criteria that reflect a tighter and more relevant industry–audience relationship.

REFERENCES

Akrim, Rashid. 2018. Online Designer on *SKAM* and *blank* at NRK P3 Event and Development, in-person interview, Oslo, 6 March.

Ang, Ien. 2005 [1991]. *Desperately Seeking the Audience*. London and New York: Routledge.

Aspeflaten, Henrik. 2017. Online Producer on *blank* and Assistant Online Producer on *SKAM* at NRK, in-person interview, Oslo, 27 September.

Baldwin, Marl W., and John G. Holmes. 1987. Salient Private Audiences and Awareness of the Self. *Journal of Personality and Social Psychology* 52 (6): 1087–1098.

Baym, Nancy. 2000. *Tune In, Log On: Fandom and Online Community*. Thousand Oaks, CA: Sage Publications.

blank. NRK. 2018–2019.

Bore, Inger-Lise Kalviknes. 2017. *Screen Comedy and Online Audiences*. London: Routledge.

Bourdon, Jérôme, and Cécile Méadel. 2014a. Deconstructing the Ratings Machine: An introduction. In *Television Audiences across the World: Deconstructing the Ratings Machine*, eds. Jérôme Bourdon and Cécile Méadel, 1–30. Basingstoke: Palgrave Macmillan.

———, eds. 2014b. *Television Audiences across the World: Deconstructing the Ratings Machine*. Basingstoke: Palgrave Macmillan.

Bruun, Hanne. 2020. *Re-Scheduling Television in the Digital Era*. London and New York: Routledge.

Busse, Kristina. 2007. Podcast and the Fun Experience of Disseminated Media Comment. https://kbusse.wordpress.com/2007/05/01/my-presentation-for-flow-2006/

Cavicchi, Daniel. 1998. *Tramps Like Us: Music and Meaning among Springsteen Fans*. New York: Oxford University Press.

Ellis, John. 2000. *Seeing Things. Television in the Age of Uncertainty*. London: I.B. Tauris.

Erlandsen, Kim. 2017. Online Developer on *SKAM* and *blank* at NRK P3 Event and Development, in-person interview, Oslo, 30 November.

———. 2018. *SKAM* Statistic—Likes and Comments on Blog. Information Given in a Meeting at the NRK, Oslo, Norway, 21 March.

Ettema, James S., and D. Charles Whitney. 1994a. The Money Arrow: An Introduction to Audiencemaking. In *Audiencemaking: How the Media Create the Audience*, eds. James S. Ettema and D. Charles Whitney, 1–18. London: Sage Publication.

———, eds. 1994b. *Audiencemaking: How the Media Create the Audience*. London: Sage Publication.

Evans, Elizabeth. 2011. *Transmedia Television*. New York: Routledge.

———. 2020. *Understanding Engagement in Transmedia Culture*. London and New York: Routledge.

Faldalen, Jon Inge. 2016. -Nerven i 'Skam' skal være sterk og relevant. *Rushprint. no*, 4 April.

Fossbakken, Tore. 2018. Post Producer on *SKAM* and *blank* at NRK, in-person interview, Oslo, 26 June.

Furevold-Boland, Marianne. 2016. Project Leader on *SKAM* at NRK, in-person interview, Oslo, 13 December.

Gray, Jonathan. 2003. New Audiences, New Textualities: Anti-fans and Non-fans. *International Journal of Cultural Studies* 6 (1): 64–81.

———. 2010. *Show Sold Separately. Promos, Spoilers, and Other Media Paratexts.* New York: New York University Press.

Gray, Jonathan, Cornel Sandvoss, and C. Lee Harrington. 2007. Introduction: Why Study Fans? In *Fandom: Identities and Communities in a Mediated World*, eds. Jonathan Gray, Cornel Sandvoss, and C. Lee Harrington, 1–16. New York: New York University Press.

Gulliksen, Hildri. 2017. Head of NRK Super, in-person interview, Oslo, 19 May.

Harrington, C. Lee, and Denis D. Bielby. 1995. *Soap Fans. Pursuing Pleasure and Making Meaning in Everyday Life.* Philadelphia: Temple University Press.

Haugen, Vibeke Fürst. 2015. Head of Programming at NRK, in-person interview, Oslo, 22 May.

Hedemann, Ole. 2014. *Ideutvikling i mediehuset.* Kristiansand: IJ-Forlaget.

———. 2017. Head of International Formats at NRK, in-person interview, Oslo, 10 November.

Hill, Annette. 2019. *Media Experiences. Engaging with Drama and Reality Television.* London and New York: Routledge.

Hill, Annette, and Jeanette Steemers. 2017. Media Industries and Engagement. *Media Industries* 4 (1): 1–5.

Hills, Matt. 2002. *Fan Cultures.* London and New York: Routledge.

Hole, Åse Marie. 2017. Project Leader on *blank* at NRK, in-person interview, Oslo, 29 September.

Jenkins, Henry. 1992. *Textual Poachers: Television Fans and Participatory Culture.* New York: Routledge.

———. 2006. *Convergence Culture. Where Old and New Media Collide.* New York and London: New York University Press.

Jensen, Jolie. 1992. Fandom as Pathology: The Consequences of Characterization. In *The Adoring Audience. Fan Culture and Popular Media*, ed. Lisa A. Lewis, 9–29. London & New York: Routledge.

Jensen, Pia Majbritt, and Ushma Chauhan Jacobsen, eds. 2020. *The Global Audiences of Danish Television Drama.* Göteborg: Nordicom.

Jenter/Girls. NRK. 2013–2018.

Johansson, Caroline Ulvin. 2020. *En bølge av tenåringsdramaer på nett. Konstruksjon av ung identitet i NRKs digital undomsserier.* Master thesis. Oslo: University of Oslo.

Johnson, Catherine. 2019. *Online TV.* London and New York: Routledge.

Køhn, Ivar. 2017. Head of NRK Drama, in-person interview, Oslo, 29 November.

Kuhn, Annette. 2012. *An Everyday Magic: Cinema and Cultural Memory.* London: I.B. Tauris.

Lang-Ree, Kari Anne. 2017. In-house Lawyer at NRK, in-person interview, Oslo, 27 October.

Lilyhammer. Rubicon TV for NRK and Netflix. 2012–2014.

Lindtner, Synnøve Skarsbø, and John Magnus Dahl. 2019. Aligning Adolescent to the Public Sphere: The Teen Serial *Skam* and Democratic Aesthetic. *Javnost—The Public* 26 (1): 54–69.

Lindtner, Synnøve Skarsbø, and John Magnus Ragnhildson Dahl. 2020. The Romantic Fantasy of Even and Isak—An Exploration of Scandinavian Women Looking for Gratification in the Teen Serial *SKAM*. *Feminist Media Studies*. Online first. https://doi.org/10.1080/14680777.2020.1830146.

Litt, Eden. 2012. Knock, Knock. Who's There? The Imagined Audience. *Journal of Broadcasting & Electronic Media* 56 (3): 330–345.

Litt, Eden, and Eszter Hargittai. 2016. The Imagined Audience on Social Network Sites. *Social Media + Society* 2 (1): 1–12.

Lotz, Amanda D. 2007. *The Television Will Be Revolutionized*. New York: New York University Press.

———. 2018. *We Now Disrupt This Broadcast. How Cable Transformed Television and the Internet Revolutionized it All*. Cambridge: The MIT Press.

Lovleg/Legal. Rubicon TV for NRK. 2018–2019.

Lund, Øyvind. 2015. Head of Media at NRK, in-person interview, Oslo, 4 February.

Magnus, Mari. 2017. Online Producer on *SKAM*, in-person interview, Oslo, 12 January.

Marwick, Alice E., and danah boyd. 2010. 'I Tweet Honestly, I Tweet Passionately': Twitter Users, Context Collapse, and the Imagined Audience. *New Media & Society* 13 (1): 114–133.

MIA. NRK. 2010–2012.

Næsheim, Knut. 2017. Director and Writer (Showrunner) on *blank* at NRK, in-person interview, Oslo, 27 September.

———. 2018. Director and Writer (Showrunner) on *blank* Season 1 at NRK, in-person interview, Oslo, 2 July.

Napoli, Philip M. 2003. *Audience Economics. Media Institutions and the Audience Marketplace*. New York: Columbia University Press.

———. 2011. *Audience Evolution. New Technologies and the Transformation of Media Audiences*. New York: Columbia University Press.

Nordlie, Hege Gaarder. 2018. Assistant Scriptwriter on *blank* at NRK, in-person interview, Oslo, 28 June.

Øverlie, Tom. 2017. Online Developer on *SKAM* and *blank* at NRK P3 Event and Development, in-person interview, Oslo, 5 December.

Pearson, Roberta. 2010. Fandom in the Digital Era. *Popular Communication* 8 (1): 84–95.

Petersen, Line Nybro, and Vilde Schanke Sundet. 2019. Play Moods across the Life Course in *SKAM* Fandom. *Journal of Fandom Studies* 7 (2): 113–131.

Rønning, Tone C. 2015. Head of Drama at NRK External and Executive Producer on *Lilyhammer*, in-person interview, Oslo, 27 January.

Sandvoss, Cornel. 2005. *Fans: The Mirror of Consumption*. Cambridge: Polity Press.

Sara. NRK. 2008–2009.

Selim, Tarek. 2017. Casting Coordinator on *blank* at NRK, in-person interview, Oslo, 23 November.

SKAM/SHAME. NRK. 2015–2017.

Sørensen, Håkon Lund. 2017. Television Analysist at NRK, in-person interview, Oslo, 13 September.

———. 2019. SKAM Statistic. Internal Document Given by E-mail, 7 May.

Sundet, Vilde Schanke. 2016. Still 'Desperately Seeking the Audience'? Audience Making in the Age of Media Convergence (the *Lilyhammer* Experience). *Northern Lights* 14 (1): 11–27.

———. 2017. 'Det er bare du som kan føle det du føler' – emosjonell investering og engasjement i nettdramaet *SKAM*. *16:9 Filmtidsskrift*.

———. 2019. From Secret Online Teen Drama to International Cult Phenomenon: The Global Expansion of *SKAM* and its Public Service Mission. *Critical Studies in Television* 15(1): 69-90.

Sundet, Vilde Schanke, and Espen Ytreberg. 2009. Working Notions of Active Audiences: Further Research on the Active Participant in Convergent Media Industries. *Convergence* 15 (4): 383–390.

Sundet, Vilde Schanke, and Line Nybro Petersen. 2020. Ins and Outs of Transmedia Fandom: Motives for Entering and Exiting the *SKAM* Fan Community Online. *Poetics*. Online first. https://doi.org/10.1016/j.poetic.2020.101510.

Syvertsen, Trine. 1997. *Den store tv-krigen. Norsk allmennfjernsyn 1988–96.* Bergen: Fagbokforlaget.

———. 2004. Citizens, Audiences, Customers and Player: A Conceptual Discussion of the Relationship between Broadcasters and their Publics. *European Journal of Cultural Studies* 7 (3): 363–380.

Tolonen, Kristian. 2015. Head of Audience Insight at NRK, in-person interview, Oslo, 6 February.

Twin Peaks. ABC. 1990–1991.

Waade, Anne Marit, Eva Novrup Redvall, and Pia Majbritt Jensen. 2020. Transnational Television Drama? Lessons Learned from Danish Drama. In *Danish Television Drama. Global Lessons from a Small Nation*, eds. Anne Marit Waade, Eva Novrup Redvall and Pia Majbritt Jensen, 1–22. London: Palgrave.

Wallace, Petter. 2015. Head of External Productions at NRK, in-person interview, Oslo, 15 January.

Whetmore, Edward J., and Alfred P. Kielwasser. 1983. The Soap Opera Audience Speaks: A Preliminary Report. *Journal of American Culture* 6: 110–116.

Williams, Raymond. 1961. *Culture and Society.* Harmondsworth: Penguin.

———. 2005 [1974]. *Television: Technology and Cultural Form.* London: Routledge.

Williams, Rebecca. 2015. *Post-Object Fandom. Television, Identify and Self-Narrative.* New York: Bloomsbury.

X-Files. FOX. 1993–2002.

CHAPTER 6

The End of Television and the New Beginning?

Abstract This chapter compares and contrasts aspects of television streaming and especially its impact on television-related practices, particularly involving quality drama series. It frames streaming in terms of the three key topics—television in a global world, television drama in the public interest and the end of television—and demonstrates how new digital production cultures, publishing models and industry–audience relations enable more flexible storytelling techniques, new production models and new publishing strategies. It also contests the argument that television is dying or that the 'love affair' between the industry and its audience has ended.

Keywords Public service television • Streaming • Television drama • Television studies • The end of television • Transnational television

INTRODUCTION

I began this book by referring to an NRK informant who feared that the long 'love affair' between the public service broadcaster and its audience was coming to an end, thanks to a changing television market with, perhaps, too many suitors (Wallace interviewed 2015). For this informant and many others, television streaming is not simply a matter of new technology or business models but a stake to the heart of traditional television production, publishing and storytelling, and of the crucial relationship

V. S. Sundet, *Television Drama in the Age of Streaming*, https://doi.org/10.1007/978-3-030-66418-3_6

129

between the industry and the audience. I have considered this position throughout this book, but the questions remain: Are we witnessing the end of a love affair? Is television drama coming to a close?

This book has engaged with television drama in the age of streaming—a time when television has been reshaped for both national and international audiences to be consumed via both linear 'flow' and on-demand user modes. Through the lens of the Norwegian public service broadcaster (NRK) and some of its game-changing drama productions (*Lilyhammer, SKAM* and *blank*), this book has analysed and discussed the impacts of recent trends within the industry on the production and release of television drama, as well as the relationship between various types of industry players—national and international, public and private—and between the industry and its audiences and fans. This book has proven that streaming brings with it both opportunities and challenges for the television industry, and that industry players such as NRK are doing their best to take advantage of those opportunities and meet those challenges. A key argument has been that television streaming *favours* a certain set of digital production cultures, publishing models and industry–audience relations which necessitate more flexible storytelling techniques, production models, publishing strategies and audience approaches. Streaming does not necessarily put other models on hold, but it aligns with some models more readily while inviting innovation, experimentation and new ways of thinking about this work. As the shifts addressed in this book indicate, streaming is far from monolithic in its nature or impact, and it is not easily defined, discussed or analysed. Furthermore, streaming looks different in different part of the world, and discussions about the changing nature of television therefore need to be studied and addressed within specific and cultural contexts (Enli and Syvertsen 2016). The aim of this book has been to provide a selection of in-depth cases involving ongoing change, but also to document a crucial period of transition in the history of television in a way which might inform the times to come, as seen from such a specific cultural context.

TELEVISION DRAMA IN A GLOBAL WORLD

In a global world, national television is increasingly put to the test. As analysed in this book, such a tension between national and global interests and players is reflected on many levels, from industry perceptions on how streaming sets up a new 'world championship' of television drama to the demand for new production and publishing models, as well as in tighter and more relevant industry–audience relations. In short, a more globalised television market increases the competition faced by national players and makes it fiercer. International streaming services provide high-quality ('world-class') content which is attractive to the audience but sets an impossible bar for national television players competing for audiences (and, increasingly, storytellers) in a global market. That said, this global market *also* accommodates the more localised content of national players—the competition becomes tougher, but the world grows smaller. Hence, this book concludes—in line with other scholars—that the international flow of power and control is not one way only but dynamic and complex, encompassing both counter-flows and sub-flows as well as room for the content of small nations like Norway (Weissmann 2012; see also Hills et al. 2019; Jensen and Jacobsen 2020). Both *Lilyhammer* and *SKAM* are good examples of (initially) small 'national' series which transcended their national boundaries to gain international value and relevance and, importantly, impact on global television trends. This is important to note in the context of a popular discourse which insists that global streaming services are 'taking over' the world. While services such as Netflix have gained key positions in many national markets, the corresponding national players have responded to the increased competition by rethinking their strategies and adapting to a new market (see also Lobato 2019).

The cases included in this book also demonstrate that international markets and partners can be reached in different ways and through various routes, again indicating the complexity of the new streaming context. Today's television market is crowded with a complex web of 'pathways', to use Annette Hill's (2019) term. For example, whereas Netflix and Red Arrow exported *Lilyhammer* internationally, teens and online fan communities were the first to export *SKAM* beyond Norway. In both cases, as well, this international expansion impacted these series in their national context by empowering them at home based on their renown abroad. *Lilyhammer*'s position in Norway, that is, was enhanced by the fact that it represented a new form of partnership with Netflix which garnered a lot of attention, nationally and internationally. Similarly, *SKAM* benefitted from the attention it received from fans and news media beyond its national borders. Despite the associated challenges and costs, the international expansion of these series undoubtedly fortified their reputations as success stories. Furthermore, both series met with international success *because* of their local distinctiveness and authenticity. While close cultural proximity and cultural authenticity was seen as a key selling point in the national context, precisely these show's 'Norwegianness' or 'difference-ness' was selling them abroad. This indicates, in turn, that local relevance and both cultural *and* transcultural proximity (Jacobsen and Jensen 2020) represent selling points in the global streaming market. These series and others like them extend the notion of success in the global television industry to encompass alternative storylines and low-budget drama which still manage to qualify as 'world class'.

Television Drama in the Public's Interest

In a global streaming world, also, public service television is put to the test. As analysed in this book, the tension between public and private services and players is reflected in many ways and echoes profound sociocultural discussions on public service (see also Flew et al. 2016). In short, a streaming television market impacts how public service institutions address their audiences, produce their drama series and publish these series—but, moreover, it also impacts the type of drama being produced in the first place. This book demonstrates, for example, that NRK has converted a more globalised television market into an argument for rethinking the idea of what it means to be a public service broadcaster, giving rise to strategies wherein value, relevance and national (or local) familiarity have significant weight. As the demand for television drama continues to increase, NRK must make its offerings more distinct, more relevant and more 'public service' oriented, but they must *also* be popular and entertaining. NRK has stressed the importance of doing this through as many distribution platforms as necessary to achieve the broadest penetration for its public service content. In short, NRK's main strategy is to produce drama series which build on audience insights to best reflect the Norwegian identity, language and culture, then share these stories using a flexible approach to both publishing platforms and models.

A key argument of this book is that the Nordic approach to public service—which allows its institutions to be both popular and flexible in the fulfilment of their missions—results in a production culture which is well suited to the creation of innovative, world-class drama, including both prime-time Nordic noir–inspired series such as *Lilyhammer* and smaller, more niche-oriented online drama series such as *SKAM* (and *blank*). Hence, this book supports the argument, also put forward by other researchers of public service institutions, that these broadcasters demonstrate great resilience amid great change in their markets (Bruun 2020; Syvertsen et al. 2014; see also Evens and Donders 2018; Redvall 2013). As Hanne Bruun writes, public service television has 'proven to be very adaptive, flexible and pragmatic throughout television history' (2020: 15). While many critics continue to insist that public service media is regularly outdone by private media, this book finds the Norwegian public broadcaster to be surprisingly successful and competitive in both national and international markets. In fact, NRK is so successful that national private television players repeatedly criticise NRK for being *too* popular and successful in its expansions into new streaming services. Although this problem is real for private players and needs to be taken seriously, it is no doubt a great benefit for Norwegian citizens and audiences to have a public service institution that manages to produce and publish attractive and high-quality television drama in an increasingly globalised and competitive television market.

Despite increased competition from international streaming services during the ten years of this analysis, NRK retained its market position and cultural relevance in Norway and even managed to launch some of its key productions internationally. Admittedly, NRK has lost some ground to services such as Netflix, and success today is no guarantee of success tomorrow, but for the moment, it remains a celebrated national provider of high-quality television drama in the digital era. It may even prove that stable public funding, a broad mission, flexible production and publishing models, and a popular approach to cultural enlightenment represent a solid foundation for success in a streaming world. Whereas the television industry and 'television' itself is changing, dynamic and flexible media institutions are changing too.

THE END OF TELEVISION DRAMA?

Based on the previous discussions, is television coming to an end? From a theoretical perspective, different perceptions of change activate different explanatory models for understanding current trends and developments. For instance, if one sees change as unexpected and comprehensive, one will seek entirely new theoretical concepts and frameworks. If, on the other hand, one sees change as anticipated, incremental and ongoing, one will instead revisit existing concepts and frameworks, testing them in the context of the change. In this book, several terms have been used and revisited, such as flow, liveness, eventfulness, paratexts and audience making, to the great benefit of the analysis of television production, publishing and consumption today. For example, flow and liveness mean very different things in a streaming world, but they are no less relevant to explain both challenges and opportunities. In fact, throughout this book, I have argued for the value of these terms as labels of core aspects of television as a medium which are not bound to technology, business models or distribution. Instead, they demonstrate the continuity of television as a medium and its inherent resilience. Hanne Bruun observes, 'In the theoretical conceptualisation of television not only change but also continuity and sustainability need to be considered if we want to understand and contribute to a re-formulated television theory for the digital age' (2020: 15).

So, are we witnessing an end of a 'love affair', as one of the informants put it? As the analyses and case studies in this book have shown, the relationship between the television industry and its audience is changing, and this change is fundamental and multifaceted. It makes the work of attracting and keeping the audience harder; it requires more flexible production and publishing models; and it rewards drama series which are promoted well, either organically or through a host of platforms and windows. However, nothing in the study indicates that television is coming to an end or that the relationship between the industry and the audience is ending. Rather the opposite, many of the cases analysed in this book are proof of a particular, strong and deep relationship between some members of the audience and their favourite television shows, including favourite characters, actors and showrunners. Besides, applying an extended definition of television—not bound to linear broadcasting but incorporating also other form of 'streaming television' and 'online television' (Johnson 2019)—proves that television is consumed more than ever. Some studies even highlight the renewed importance of television as a 'safe space' in periods of turmoil and uncertainty, addressing how audiences turn to the television screen for both companionship and an escape from worrying realities (Johnson and Dempsey 2020). As such, the 'love affair' between the industry and its audience is changing, but the partners remain committed.

REFERENCES

blank. NRK. 2018–2019.

Bruun, Hanne. 2020. *Re-Scheduling Television in the Digital Era.* London and New York: Routledge.

Enli, Gunn, and Trine Syvertsen. 2016. The End of television—Again! How TV Is Still Influenced by Cultural Factors in the Age of Digital Intermediaries. *Media and Communication* 4 (3): 142–153.

Evens, Tom, and Karen Donders. 2018. *Platform Power and Policy in Transforming Television Markets.* Cham, Switzerland: Palgrave Macmillan.

Flew, Terry, Petros Iosifidis, and Jeanette Steemers, eds. 2016. *Global Media and National Policies.* London: Palgrave Macmillan.

Hill, Annette. 2019. *Media Experiences. Engaging with Drama and Reality Television.* London and New York: Routledge.

Hills, Matt, Michele Hilmes, and Roberta Pearson, eds. 2019. *Transatlantic Television Drama. Industries, Programmes, & Fans.* Oxford: Oxford University Press.

Jacobsen, Ushma Chauhan, and Pia Majbritt Jensen. 2020. Unfolding the Global Travel of Danish Television Drama Series. In *The Global Audiences of Danish Television Drama,* eds. Pia Majbritt Jensen and Ushma Chauhan Jacobsen, 9–19. Göteborg: Nordicom.

Jensen, Pia Majbritt, and Ushma Chauhan Jacobsen, eds. 2020. *The Global Audiences of Danish Television Drama.* Göteborg: Nordicom.

Johnson, Catherine. 2019. *Online TV.* London and New York: Routledge.

Johnson, Catherine, and Lauren Dempsey. 2020. How Coronavirus Might have Changed TV Viewing Habits for Good—New Research. *The Conversation,* 11 November.

Lilyhammer. Rubicon TV for NRK and Netflix. 2012–2014.

Lobato, Ramon. 2019. *Netflix Nations. The Geography of Digital Distribution.* New York: New York University Press.

Redvall, Eva Novrup. 2013. *Writing and Producing Television Drama in Denmark: From the Kingdom to the Killing.* Hampshire: Palgrave Macmillan.

SKAM/SHAME. NRK. 2015–2017.

Syvertsen, Trine, Gunn Enli, Ole J. Mjøs, and Hallvard Moe. 2014. *The Media Welfare State: Nordic Media in the Digital Era.* Ann Arbor: University of Michigan Press.

Wallace, Petter. 2015. Head of External Productions at NRK, in-person interview, Oslo, 15 January.

Weissmann, Elke. 2012. *Transnational Television Drama: Special Relations and Mutual Influence between the US and UK.* New York: Palgrave Macmillan.

Appendix: Industry Informants

Informants are listed alphabetically with the title and affiliation they had at the time of the interview.

Akrim, Rashid, Online Designer on *SKAM* and *blank* at NRK P3 Event and Development, in-person interview, Oslo, 6 March 2018 and 28 June 2018.

Andressen, Anne, Editor on *blank* at NRK, in-person interview, Oslo, 28 May 2018 and 26 June 2018.

Arnø, William Greni, Actor on *blank* at NRK, in-person interview, Oslo, 28 June 2018.

Aspeflaten, Henrik, Online Producer on *blank* and Assistant Online Producer on *SKAM* at NRK, in-person interview, Oslo, 27 September 2017 and 26 June 2018.

Bettvik, Ida, Production Leader on *SKAM* (S4) and *blank* at NRK, in-person interview, Oslo, 24 November 2017 and 26 June 2018.

Bjørn, Camilla, Head of NRK P3, in-person interview, Oslo, 23 March 2018.

Bjørnstad, Anne, Showrunner on *Lilyhammer* at Rubicon TV, in-person interview, Oslo, 18 February 2015.

Conesa, Cecilie Amlie, Actor on *blank* at NRK, in-person interview, Oslo, 28 June 2018.

Eriksen, Thor Germund, Broadcasting Director at NRK, in-person interview, Oslo, 14 March 2018.

© The Author(s), under exclusive license to Springer Nature Switzerland AG 2021
V. S. Sundet, *Television Drama in the Age of Streaming*,
https://doi.org/10.1007/978-3-030-66418-3

Erlandsen, Kim, Online Developer on *SKAM* and *blank* at NRK P3 Event and Development, in-person interview, Oslo, 30 November 2017 and 28 June 2018.

Flesjø, Nicolay, Editorial Director of On-Demand Services at NRK, in-person interview, Oslo, 26 January 2015.

Folkestad, Mattis, Online Developer on *SKAM* and *blank* at NRK P3 Event and Development, in-person interview, Oslo, 28 June 2018.

Forsberg, Sara, Chief Property Master on *blank* at NRK, in-person interview, Oslo, 22 December 2017 and 26 June 2018.

Fort, Jakob Larsen, Actor on *blank* at NRK, in-person interview, Oslo, 28 June 2018.

Fossbakken, Tore, Post Producer on *SKAM* and *blank* at NRK, in-person interview, Oslo, 29 November 2017 and 26 June 2018.

Furevold-Boland, Marianne, Project Leader on *SKAM* at NRK, in-person interview, Oslo, 13 December 2016.

Gulliksen, Hildri, Head of NRK Super, in-person interview, Oslo, 19 May 2017.

Haugen, Vibeke Fürst, Head of Programming at NRK, in-person interview, Oslo, 22 May 2015.

Hedemann, Ole, Head of International Formats at NRK, in-person interview, Oslo, 9 April 2015 and 10 November 2017.

Helsingen, Arne, Head of Television at NRK, in-person interview, Oslo, 16 January 2015.

Hole, Åse Marie, Project Leader on *blank* at NRK, in-person interview, Oslo, 29 September 2017, 17 January 2018, 28 June 2018 and 2 July 2018.

Køhn, Ivar, Head of NRK Drama, in-person interview, Oslo, 29 November 2017.

Kolbjørnsen, Anne, Head of Script at Rubicon TV and executive producer on *Lilyhammer*, in-person interview, Oslo, 27 March 2015.

Kristiansen, Pål Kruke, CEO of Rubicon TV and executive producer on *Lilyhammer*, in-person interview, Oslo, 21 January 2015.

Landa, Mira Genevieve Dagbo, Property Master on *blank* at NRK, in-person interview, Oslo, 26 June 2018.

Lang-Ree, Kari Anne, In-house Lawyer at NRK, in-person interview, Oslo, 27 October 2017.

Lund, Øyvind, Head of Media at NRK, in-person interview, Oslo, 4 February 2015.

Magnus, Mari, Online Producer on *SKAM*, in-person interview, Oslo, 12 January 2017.

Maurud, Johan Hveem, Actor on *blank* at NRK, in-person interview, Oslo, 28 June 2018.

Melhø, Karine Brøste, Head of Casting on *blank* at NRK, in-person interview, Oslo, 23 November 2017.

Molstad, Ragnar, Photographer on *SKAM* (S3) and *blank* at NRK, in-person interview, Oslo, 21 December 2017 and 26 June 2018.

Næsheim, Knut, Director and Writer (Showrunner) on *blank* Season 1 at NRK, in-person interview, Oslo, 27 September 2017, 23 April 2018 and 2 July 2018.

Nordlie, Hege Gaarder, Assistant Scriptwriter on *blank* at NRK, in-person interview, Oslo, 6 December 2017 and 28 June 2018.

Olsen, Linn-Agnete, First Assistant Director and Coordinator on *blank* at NRK, in-person interview, Oslo, 26 June 2018.

Øverlie, Tom, Online Developer on *SKAM* and *blank* at NRK P3 Event and Development, in-person interview, Oslo, 5 December 2017 and 28 June 2018.

Rønning, Tone C., Head of Drama at NRK External and executive producer on *Lilyhammer*, in-person interview, Oslo, 27 January 2015.

Selim, Tarek, Casting Coordinator on *blank* at NRK, in-person interview, Oslo, 23 November 2017 and 26 June 2018.

Skodvin, Eilif, Showrunner on *Lilyhammer* at Rubicon TV, in-person interview, Oslo, 18 February 2015.

Sørensen, Håkon Lund, Television Analyst at NRK, in-person interview, Oslo, 13 September 2017.

Sprus, Nathalie, NRK's Press Contact on *SKAM* and *blank* at NRK, in-person interview, Oslo, 19 February 2018.

Svae-Johansen, Cathrine, Editor on *blank* at NRK, in-person interview, Oslo, 28 May 2018 and 26 June 2018.

Thorsby, Marte, Managing Director at IFPI Norge, in-person interview, Oslo, 8 November 2017.

Tolonen, Kristian, Head of Audience Insight at NRK, in-person interview, Oslo, 6 February 2015.

Unger, Kirsten, Recording Audio on *blank* at NRK, in-person interview, Oslo, 26 June 2018.

Wallace, Petter, Head of External Productions at NRK, in-person interview, Oslo 15 January 2015.

Wisløff, Anne, Showrunner on *Sara, Mia, Jenter, LikMeg* at NRK Super, in-person interview, Oslo, 9 March 2018.

Index[1]

[1] Note: Page numbers followed by 'n' refer to notes.

© The Author(s), under exclusive license to Springer Nature
Switzerland AG 2021
V. S. Sundet, *Television Drama in the Age of Streaming*,
https://doi.org/10.1007/978-3-030-66418-3